The New Self-Care:

A Playbook for Money Mindset Reset

The New Self Care: A Playbook for Money Mindset Reset

For permission requests, please contact the publisher by email at:
support@wisemindsshop.org

Identifiers: Library of Congress: 2025903520 | ISBN: 978-1-966514-00-8 (paperback)

Published by: Wise Minds

Any references to historical events, real people, or real places are used fictitiously. This book is intended for informational and educational purposes only and should not be considered financial or legal advice. Readers should consult a qualified professional before making financial decisions.

First Edition

Printed in the United States of America

This Book Belongs To :

Table of Contents

Instructions ---------- 5

Section 1: The Healthy Definition of Money ---------- 7

Section 2: The Root of your Money Beliefs ---------- 19

Section 3: Redefining Financial Values Your Own Way ---------- 29

Section 4: Appreciating What You Have And Using It ---------- 49

Section 5: Stewarding Your Money Well ---------- 65

Budget Template ---------- 67

Section 6: What to Do If (And When) ---------- 87

Section 7: The Habitual Practice of Self-Applause ---------- 111

Celebration Ideas ---------- 133

Savings Tips ---------- 136

Upcoming Goals & Steps ---------- 140

How to Use This Playbook

Hey there, gorgeous! ❤

First off, thank you for believing in yourself (we love to see it!) and trusting us by picking up The New Self-Care: A Playbook for Money Mindset Reset. This isn't just another money mindset book—it's your space to dream big, reflect deeply, and grow into the version of yourself who takes control of her finances with confidence and intention.

So why call it "The New Self-Care"? Because self-care isn't just about bubble baths and face masks, even though those are very much so needed. True self-care is about living with intention, aligning your actions with your goals, and creating a life that feels as good as it looks. That's the message we're trying to get across here.

So let's get into it!

First Off, Take Your Time

Sis, remember these words whenever you start to feel discouraged: progress isn't about speed–it's about depth. Finishing this playbook isn't a race, it's a journey. So take your time with each section. If a prompt, activity, or challenge feels heavy, it's okay to put the playbook down for a day or two and come back to it when you're ready. Each page is designed to help you dig deep and reimagine how you think about money. There's no deadline for growth, so let the process unfold naturally.

Engage with Every Page

This isn't just a book you read; it's a book you live. Whether it's a journal prompt, a financial challenge, or a fun Mad Libs activity, every single page has been written with a purpose. Feel like skipping something? Ask yourself why. Do you feel resistance? Discomfort? (Or hey, maybe you're just not feeling it–and that's okay). Lean into those feelings. They're often the key to unlocking something bigger & deeper.

Make It Your Own

This is your space! Write, doodle, highlight, slap some sticky notes on a page–whatever helps you connect with the material better. This playbook is here to meet you where you are and grow with you. So don't be shy–get creative and be unapologetically you.

Have Fun and Find Peace

Growth isn't a chore; it's an upgrade. Celebrate every win, enjoy the playful sections, and let yourself soak in the peace that comes with taking control of your financial mindset. It's not just about the end goal–it's about enjoying the process too.

We're Listening

Your experience matters to us. As you work through this playbook, we'd love to hear from you. Did you love a certain page? Was there a prompt that hit just right? Do you think something could be even better?

Your helpful feedback isn't just about improving this playbook–it's about fueling a movement. Together, we can create tools that empower more women to step out of survival mode and into a life of intention, confidence, and peace. So don't hold back. Share your thoughts at www.wisemindsshop.org and let's lift each other up!

Alright, girlfriend, let's do this!

Section 1:
The Healthy Definition of Money

Hey girl, this concept might be very unorthodox and most likely very different from the other money mindset books you've read. However, here's the truth about money that no one really talks about: money isn't the goal. It's not the dream. It's not even the finish line.

Money is the tool. It's the hammer in your hand, the paintbrush on your canvas, the helper to your future. But here's the kicker... it only works when you do.
Think about it. Every dollar you touch has a purpose, whether you decide to use it or not. It can pay for a single meal or be an investment that feeds your future for years. It can create stress if it's spent recklessly, or peace if it's handled intentionally.

The difference isn't in the money itself - it's in you!

Money doesn't care who you are or where you came from. It's class-neutral. It's not impressed by designer labels; it's not ashamed of thrift store finds. What matters is **how you will use it.** Will you let it slip through your fingers, or will you direct it toward something meaningful?

Your money is already working—it's just a matter of whether it's working for you or against you. The power lies within your hands & your mind. Every dollar is a choice, a tool, a tiny little soldier you send out into the world to fight for the life you want. Once you understand this, you can never unlearn it.

Your money is your power. And, honey, it's time to take it back.

So here are some transformative words to help reshape your mindset...

Instead of the words on the left, try using the words on the right. Notice the difference in emotion when you use these transformative words.

Perfection → Progress

Stop chasing perfection. It's progress that moves the needle

Goals → Growth

Goals are important, but **true** success lies in ongoing growth.

Wealth → Wellness

Money isn't just about wealth. It's about creating financial wellness.

Control → Alignment

Instead of trying to control everything, focus on aligning your money with your values.

Sacrifice → Choice

It's not about sacrificing joy, but choosing what **truly** matters to you.

Hustle → Intentionality

Hustle culture glorifies exhaustion, but intentionality celebrates purpose.

Budget → Blueprint

A budget isn't restrictive, it's your blueprint for the life you want.

Spending → Investing

Every dollar spent is an investment in something. It's up to you what it's investing in.

Success → Sustainability

Success isn't just achieving something once; it's creating sustainable habits.

Conservation → Freedom

Conservation isn't about depriving yourself; it's about financial freedom.

Earning → Building

It's not just about earning money, it's about building a life you love.

Saving → Securing

Saving is about securing your future, not just stockpiling cash

Failure → Feedback

Financial mistakes aren't failures, they're feedback for your next move.
Try again with a better-informed move.

Success → Fulfillment

True financial success is finding fulfillment, not just reaching milestones.

Risk → Opportunity

Financial risks can be opportunities for growth when taken wisely. Don't be afraid; open your eyes to the possibilities.

Money → Tool

Money isn't the destination; it's the tool that helps you get there. Use it wisely.

Discipline → Self-control

Discipline can feel rigid and external, but self-control comes from within and empowers you to make mindful choices.

Transformative Action:

While you're reflecting on this list of transformative words, pick 1-5 words from the left that you use fairly often. Write down next to each pair how the transformative word makes you feel vs the original word and make a conscious effort to replace them with the words on the right.

Make these words a part of your **new** vocabulary because the way you think is how you feel–and how you feel is what you do. In order to change your money mindset (as redundant as it sounds), we have to change your mind. This starts with how you talk to **you.**

1. When I think about money as a tool, what kind of tool do I see it as?

Is it a hammer to build something, a key to unlock opportunities, or something else? How do you feel about the idea that you are the one holding that tool?

2. How do I currently use my money as a tool?

Identify one recent way you've spent or saved money. Was that decision intentional, emotional, or habitual? Explain how that decision made you feel —and if you feel as though you should do it again.

3. What is one small step I can take today to use my money more intentionally?

Focus on one action and one action only! This is your starting step, and you do not want to put too much on yourself at the beginning of your journey. There will be more opportunities ahead to implement more action. Trust me.

The "Goal Jar" Game

How It Works:

Identify one recent way you've spent or saved money. Was that decision intentional, emotional, or habitual? Explain how that decision made you feel—and if you feel as though you should do it again.

Why It's Fun:

- Adds an element of surprise and variety.
- Breaks bigger financial goals into bite-sized, achievable tasks.
- Keeps you engaged by mixing things up.

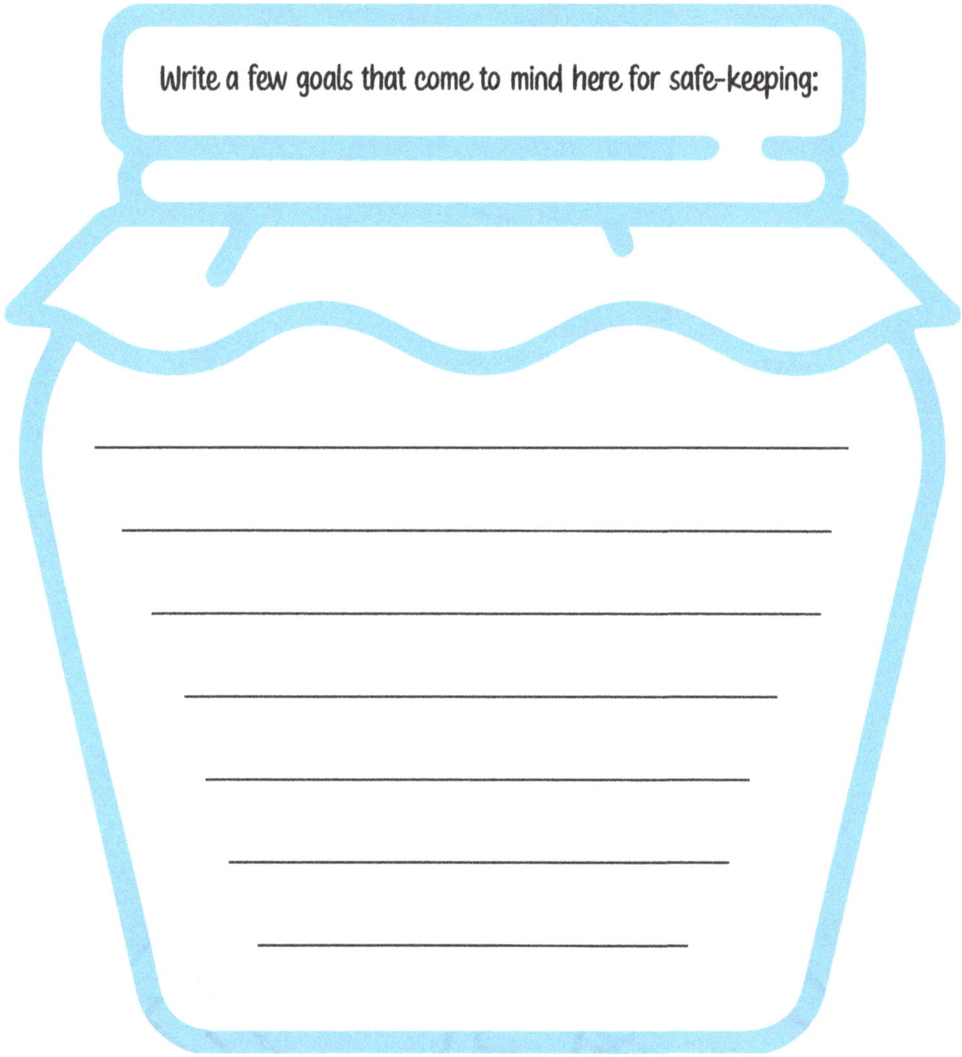

Myth-Busting Quiz:
Redefining Money

Before we dive deeper, let's bust some myths about money. You might be surprised how many common beliefs are holding you back. Answer each statement as True or False, then read the explanations to get the full picture.

1. "Having more money will solve all my problems."
True / False

2. "Debt is always bad."
True / False

3. "Budgeting means giving up the things I love."
True / False

4. "Money is the root of all evil."
True / False

5. "If I earn more money, I'll automatically save more."
True / False

6. "You have to work harder to make more money."
True / False

7. "Money will make me happy."
True / False

Answer Key + Explanations

1. FALSE

Money may solve financial problems, but it won't fix emotional or relational issues. What truly matters is how you manage and use your resources. It's not just about how much you have.

2. FALSE

Not all debt is created equal. Borrowing to invest in your education, start a business, or purchase property can build wealth. The key is managing debt wisely and not overextending yourself.

3. FALSE

A budget isn't about restriction; it's about priorities. It allows you to intentionally allocate your money toward what you truly value such as self-care, hobbies, or future goals while cutting out what doesn't align with your values.

4. FALSE

The original quote is, "The love of money is the root of all evil." Money itself is neutral. It's your intentions and actions with money that define its impact in your life.

5. FALSE

Lifestyle inflation often creeps in as income grows, leading to higher spending without intentional savings. Saving is a habit, not a byproduct of earning.

6. FALSE

Hard work is important, but working smarter by leveraging skills, networking, and seeking opportunities—often leads to greater financial success than just effort alone.

7. FALSE

While financial security can reduce stress and create temporary fun, happiness comes from purpose, relationships, and self-growth—not just your bank balance.

Oath to Self:

Viewing Money As My Tool

I declare today that money is my tool.
I will no longer view it as the goal, but a means to build the life I desire.
Every dollar I touch will reflect my values, goals, and vision for the future.

I vow to be intentional, not impulsive; mindful, not reckless.
I will see money for what it truly is: an opportunity to create freedom, peace, and purpose.

From this moment forward, I will not let fear or shame dictate my financial decisions. PERIOD.
I will take control, align my money with my values, and use it to build a life I love.

I am capable.
I am powerful.
And I will honor this truth with every choice I make.

This is my commitment to myself.
This is my promise to my future.

____

Sign here

Transformative Words
Wordsearch

S	A	H	G	E	B	L	U	E	P	R	I	N	T	E	W	S	T	O	O	L
I	U	F	G	N	I	D	L	I	U	B	C	Y	I	C	E	S	R	A	S	R
I	P	S	E	L	F	C	O	N	T	R	O	L	B	P	L	E	A	E	C	N
N	L	G	T	O	P	A	J	U	N	B	U	I	O	P	L	N	N	I	O	S
T	M	L	E	A	O	E	B	E	W	L	R	O	Y	R	N	D	S	G	N	R
E	N	O	C	D	I	H	A	S	K	J	A	H	O	P	E	N	F	T	F	E
N	A	F	D	O	A	N	O	C	J	I	G	W	J	R	S	I	O	G	I	W
T	E	E	C	E	O	R	A	H	E	J	E	F	R	J	S	K	R	T	D	O
I	D	E	N	H	E	I	C	B	H	E	R	O	H	T	G	A	M	N	E	P
O	U	D	A	C	A	R	J	S	I	N	V	E	S	T	I	N	G	E	N	M
N	T	B	A	I	E	H	F	E	T	L	O	V	E	R	A	S	N	M	C	E
A	I	A	E	R	C	I	I	D	H	E	I	O	W	L	E	R	I	N	E	V
L	T	C	R	H	I	W	P	G	R	O	W	T	H	C	I	T	R	G	M	R
I	A	K	P	R	O	G	R	E	S	S	V	E	Y	R	N	V	U	I	S	O
T	R	H	W	O	H	F	E	C	N	E	I	T	A	P	D	M	C	L	L	G
Y	G	B	R	L	C	O	P	P	O	R	T	U	N	I	T	Y	E	A	N	R
N	F	U	L	F	I	L	L	M	E	N	T	S	C	O	R	T	S	E	B	A
F	L	R	S	S	E	N	I	P	P	A	H	M	S	E	L	F	C	A	R	E

1. Progress
2. Growth
3. Self-control
4. Wellness
5. Courage
6. Alignment
7. Love
8. Choice
9. Intentionality
10. Blueprint
11. Hope
12. Investing
13. Kindness
14. Sustainability
15. Freedom
16. Joy
17. Building
18. Empower
19. Securing
20. Happiness
21. Feedback
22. Fulfillment
23. Opportunity
24. Confidence
25. Tool
26. Self-care
27. Peace
28. Patience
29. Gratitude
30. Transform

Section 2:
The Root of Your Money Beliefs

Here's something we wish more of the girls knew: your relationship with money is a mindset that starts at a young age. It starts with watching your parents struggle to make ends meet or consistently splurging on many treats, receiving your allowance when you do your chores on time or getting a little extra cash for all those A's on your report card. Then, it really sinks in when you're in highschool; coming back from Christmas break and comparing your gifts to others. It affects everyone on each side of the fence, whether you got the newest trendy item or something more "generic". Everything you've been exposed to up until now has shaped the way you think about money.

This mindset entices you to chase after goals, always in relation to money. Because what happens after you graduate from highschool? What is everyone aiming towards? A degree, then a career, then a house. We're not saying those goals are wrong, but it strongly encourages you to continue to chase after your goals to acquire more money. You know that saying, "Money is the root of all evil"? Well, money itself isn't evil–it's the obsession with it that drains your energy, takes away from your relationships, and makes you do things you thought you'd never do before (i.e. choosing work over spending time with family/friends).

So, let's talk about it–but intentionally. This may be the hardest section of this entire playbook, and we are here for you, sis. However, it's extremely important that you're honest with yourself about what has shaped your relationship with money. We're getting to the root of your trauma. So please, take your time and give yourself space to feel and understand this.

You are breaking a mental barrier here.

Okay, enough serious talk for a bit. Let's have some fun!

Wordplay Activity
"If My Money Could Talk"

Alright, girlfriend, let's spill some tea. Imagine your money sat you down for a heart-to-heart. What would it say about you? (Extra fun: give your money a name!)

"Listen up, ____________(**your name**). First of all, I've been trying to get your attention for ages, but you keep ignoring me when I'm____

____

(a financial habit, like being spent recklessly or not tracked properly).

Can we have a real convo about how we treat each other? I'm not mad at you, I'm just tired of being spent on ____

(something you overspend on, like takeout, subscriptions, or impulse buys)

GIRL, we can do better than this! I need you to take care of me like I take care of you!"

Just a heads up–your money might get a little emotional here.

"You know, I've been with you through it all–those highs when you got that

____

(something you saved up for and loved, like a vacation or dream purchase)

and those lows when ____

____

(something money-related that caused stress, like an overdraft or unexpected expense).

I love when you use me to invest in ____

(something meaningful, like personal growth, self-care, or loved ones).

It makes me feel like we're besties. But to be honest with you, I hate it when you keep __________

____

(a habit your money dislikes, like blowing your budget or skipping savings).

It's like you don't even care about how I feel!"

"Here's the thing—I see how hard you're trying, and I'm so proud of you for __________________

____

(a recent good financial move, like creating a budget or making an extra loan payment).

It's these decisions that remind me that we are doing okay. If we keep this up, I know we can get to ____

____

(a dream outcome: financial freedom, a house, a big savings account)

before you know it. You just have to trust me—and believe in yourself. We've got this!"

"Money might not buy happiness, but when we work together, we can create freedom, peace, and so much more! So let's promise each other something today: no more fear or guilt. Let's start showing up for each other in a way that feels not just good, but great. I believe in you, ______________ **(your name)**—you CAN do this and you will if you just believe in yourself!"

1. What's one money belief you grew up with that doesn't align with who you are today?

2. If money could talk, what would it say about your relationship with it?

3. Pause for a moment and think about your money. What's the first feeling that comes to mind– stress, excitement, or maybe something else?

Write down what those emotions are. Then, reflect on this: if money is just a tool or resource, how can you start seeing it as something that works for you instead of something that controls your lifestyle?

The "Expense Detective" Game

How It Works

Review your last month's bank or credit card statement and highlight or write down all of your purchases that were wants, not needs. Total them up, then challenge yourself to save 35-50% of that amount this pay period (or month).

Extra Hard Version: Save 75-100% of that amount this month.

Affirmations to Reflect On During The Challenge:

- Each dollar I save or spend wisely literally brings me a step closer to the freedom I deserve.
- My money is my financial partner, not my financial problem. I let go of any stress and embrace smart and calm decisions.
- I respect my money by giving it a place to have purpose. I spend, save, and invest intentionally.

Oath to Self:

The "Respect My Money, Respect Myself" Oath

"From this moment on, I, ___________ , declare that I WILL redefine my relationship with money. I will no longer see it as a source of stress or excitement, but as a partner that works with me.

I promise to be intentional with my spending, and recognize the difference between wants and needs. Each decision I make will reflect the respect I have for myself—whether that means saving, spending, or investing with purpose.

I commit to freeing myself from the hold of scarcity that has limited me. Instead, I will embrace an abundance mindset, knowing that money is a tool that amplifies my ability to create and live fully.

I will not measure my worth by the amount of money I have, but by the clarity and joy my financial decisions bring to me. My success is not defined by chasing numbers, but by creating a life that aligns with my values, goals, and dreams.

Today, I step into my power, ready to rewrite my story and reclaim control over my financial journey.
This is not just about money—it's about me, my future, and the mental freedom I deserve. I respect my money because I respect myself.

____

Sign here

What's Your Money Story?

Personality Quiz

Ready to uncover how your childhood shaped your money mindset? Answer these questions honestly and let's see where your story started.

1. As a kid, what was Christmas morning like for you?

A. I couldn't wait to unwrap the newest gadgets or trendy toys everyone was talking about!

B. It was exciting, but my gifts were usually practical or things I really needed.

C. I loved the traditions more than anything—spending time with family and enjoying good food.

2. In high school, how did you feel about your outfits?

A. I always had the latest brands or whatever was trending –I was a style queen!

B. I made do with what I had, but I felt pressure to keep up sometimes.

C. I wore what made me happy and didn't worry much about trends– it was all about comfort and personal style.

3. When your allowance came in, what did you do?

A. I spent it right away—candy, toys, you name it!

B. It normally went straight to my piggy bank.

C. I thoughtfully spent it on things that brought me joy.

4. Think about birthday parties growing up. What was your vibe?

A. Big party, big gifts, all my friends there–it was a full event!

B. A small gathering with close family and maybe one or two friends–it was simple yet special.

C. A mix of both–my closest friends, fun activities and moments that I'll always remember.

5. In high school, how did you feel about comparing holiday or birthday gifts with friends?

A. Confident—I usually had some of the coolest stuff.

B. Anxious—I didn't always have what others had.

C. Indifferent—I cared more about the experiences and time spent than the gifts themselves.

6. Now that you're an adult, how do you handle treating yourself?

A. If I see something I love, I get it—YOLO!

B. I hesitate or wait for a sale, even if it's something I really want.

C. I treat myself when it aligns with my values or the time is right.

7. When you look back at your childhood, what stands out most?

A. How my parents worked hard to give me everything I wanted.

B. How my parents efficiently used every dollar to make things work.

C. How we created meaningful memories through family time and simple joys.

Results:

Mostly A's: The "Treat Yourself" Giver: Your childhood was filled with abundance, which shaped your mindset around money as something to enjoy and spend freely. You love treating yourself and those you care about, but sometimes you might find it hard to save or say no to a splurge. It's all about finding balance and remembering that the best "treat" is peace of mind.

Mostly B's: The "Make It Work" Planner: Growing up, you learned the value of a dollar early. You've always known how to stretch your resources and make the most of what you have. As an adult, you probably lean toward saving and being cautious, but don't forget—it's okay to enjoy what you've earned, too. Balance is the key, bestie!

Mostly C's: The "Fulfillment Seeker": You grew up appreciating the value of life beyond money, whether it was the joy of spending time with family, exploring hobbies, or connecting with friends. You weren't overly focused on materialistic things, but instead, you found contentment in what you had, valuing experiences over possessions. Your interests often leaned toward meaningful activities like enjoying nature, being creative, or simply having fun! Trends and flashy lifestyles never defined who you are because your roots lie in seeking fulfillment through deeper connections and personal growth.

Section 3:

Redefining Financial Values Your Own Way

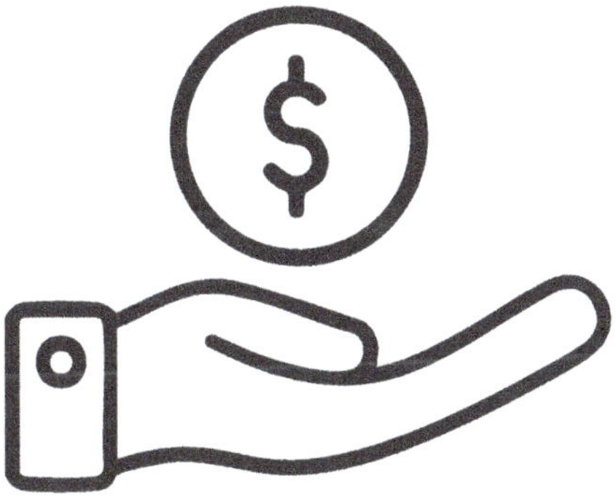

Congratulations!

You made it through the hardest part of resetting your money mindset.

How do you feel?

Just know, no matter how you feel, you're on the right track! Let's keep the ball rolling! Now that you've identified what you know to be a little toxic for your money mindset, we need to redefine what financial success means for you.

It's definitely not defined as the size of your paycheck, the number of zeros in your bank account, or the designer labels hanging in your closet. It's about creating a life that feels good for you.

So here's the tea, sis: Society loves to tell us what success should look like. Society loves to paint the picture for us, especially us women. But it's time we stand up and define success in our own lives. What's really going to make you happy and fulfilled? What do you want to do in this world? We only get one life, so what is it that you want to get out of your time here?

Let's define success on your own terms. Spoiler alert: you're going to love it here.

My Future Self Writes Me a Thank-You Letter

Dear (**your name**)________________ ,

Wow. Just wow. You did THAT! I'm sitting here in the future, sipping a ____________________(**fancy beverage**) in our dream ________________ ______________________ (**place you want to live**), and it's all thanks to the decisions you made back in ______ (**current year**).

Let me tell you what life feels like now: ______________(**emotion you want to feel about money**)—not because we have everything, but because we've learned to appreciate what matters most. You've built a life that feels good for us, one that aligns with what we value.

Remember when you chose to stop spending money on ___________________________ (**unnecessary expense**)? That small change was a huge turning point. Now, I get to enjoy _________________(**financial freedom benefit**), and let me tell you... it feels incredible.

You've set us up for success with smart moves like _______________________ ________ (**positive money habit**) and prioritizing _______________________ (**financial value**). It wasn't always easy—like the time you had to say no to ____________(**temporary sacrifice**)—but look where it got us!

Today, I look around and see more than the pieces of that dream world you envisioned back in ________(**current year**). I'm living in it.

So thank you for being disciplined, determined, and a total boss at __________________ (**successful habit**). You've proven that success isn't about chasing society's standards, it's about building one that's authentically ours.

I'm so proud of you, girlfriend!

With love and endless gratitude,

Future Me

1. Now's the time to write it all down!

What does your perfect world look like for you? What's going to make you happy & fulfilled? What do you want to achieve in this world? What do you want to do with your time here? Write it all out in full detail. No one is going to see this, and it's completely free to imagine. Go in & go off!

Continued ...

Continued ...

2. Are your goals really *that* far out of your reach?

If so, write down **why** so you know what barrier(s) you're going to smash through. Notice how we said **going to.**

The "Spend and Match" Game

How It Works

For the next 3 days, match the amount of every non-essential purchase you make (e.g., coffee, dining out, shopping) and put it into savings. If you can't afford to match it, you skip the purchase.

Extra Hard Version: Play the Spend and Match game for the next 7 days.

Why It's Fun

- Makes you pause and think before spending.
- Balances splurges with financial responsibility.
- Adds an element of self-discipline disguised as a game.

Affirmations to Reflect On During The Challenge:

- Every financial choice I make today builds a foundation for the freedom that future me deserves.
- I live with purpose and prioritize what truly matters.
- My time, energy, and money flow towards my biggest dreams.

Discover your Dream Life

Personality Quiz

1. What's your ideal Saturday morning?

A. Exploring a local market or hiking trail
B. Sleeping in, then heading to a fancy brunch
C. Volunteering or organizing a community event
D. Traveling to a new city or planning my next trip
E. Taking a yoga class or indulging in self-care

2. What's your dream vacation?

A. A cozy cabin in the mountains
B. A luxury resort with all the inclusions
C. A cultural immersion experience
D. A whirlwind tour of multiple countries on one trip
E. A wellness retreat with spa treatments and meditation

3. What's your favorite way to spend free time?

A. Gardening, cooking, or DIY projects
B. Shopping, dining out, or attending a show
C. Mentoring others or planning charity events
D. Exploring hidden gems in my own city or abroad
E. Reading, journaling, or relaxing at home

4. If you received a $10,000 bonus, what would you do with it?

A. Upgrade my home or invest in property
B. Splurge on a luxury item on my wishlist
C. Donate a portion and save the rest
D. Book an extravagant trip
E. Invest in my health or personal growth program

5. What's your dream work environment?

A. A cozy home office surrounded by plants
B. A sleek, high-rise office with a view
C. A collaborative nonprofit space full of like-minded people
D. A mobile setup that lets me work anywhere
E. A wellness-focused workplace with meditation breaks

6. What's your ultimate relationship goal?

A. A close-knit family life with strong traditions
B. A power couple vibe where we both inspire greatness
C. Giving back as a family through volunteering or charity work
D. A travel partner who shares my wanderlust
E. Building a healthy, balanced partnership full of mutual growth

7. What's your go-to comfort food?

A. Home-cooked meals made from scratch
B. Fine dining or gourmet treats
C. Whatever's available while I'm busy helping others
D. International cuisine that takes my taste buds on a trip
E. Organic or health-conscious snacks

8. What inspires you most?

A. Nature and simple living
B. Ambition and luxury
C. Helping others and leaving a legacy
D. Curiosity and a desire to see the world
E. Balance, harmony, and well-being

9. What's your favorite type of movie or TV show?

A. Heartwarming dramas or action-filled movies
B. Glamorous reality shows or high-powered thrillers
C. Stories about change-makers and community leaders
D. Travel documentaries or adventure films
E. Relaxing nature shows

10. How do you spend a lazy Sunday?

A. Working on hobbies or relaxing at home
B. Shopping or hitting up a trendy restaurant
C. Volunteering or brainstorming new ways to help others
D. Researching my next big trip or adventure
E. Practicing self-care, from bubble baths to face masks

11. What's your dream house?

A. A rustic farmhouse with plenty of space for a garden
B. A modern mansion with cutting-edge tech and style
C. A cozy yet spacious home with room for community gatherings
D. A chic apartment in the heart of a bustling city
E. A tranquil retreat surrounded by nature

12. What's your approach to fitness?

A. Outdoor activities like hiking or biking
B. Personal trainers and luxury gyms
C. Group activities like charity walks or community sports teams
D. Staying active through travel and exploration
E. Yoga, pilates, or meditation

13. What's your biggest financial goal?

A. Saving for a dream home or property investment
B. Earning enough to afford a luxury lifestyle
C. Creating a fund to support causes I'm passionate about
D. Building a flexible income that allows me to travel freely
E. Reaching financial freedom to focus on personal wellness

14. What's your social vibe?

A. Intimate gatherings with close friends
B. Glamorous parties and exclusive events
C. Community events or volunteering efforts
D. Networking events with travelers and adventurers
E. Quiet nights in or small, peaceful get-togethers outdoors

15. What's your life motto?

A. "Bloom where you're planted."
B. "Work hard, play harder."
C. "Leave the world better than you found it."
D. "Collect memories, not things."
E. "Health is wealth."

Answer Key
(Circle yours)

Mostly A's:
Homesteader's Haven

Mostly B's:
Glamorous Goal-Digger

Mostly C's:
Legacy Builder

Mostly D's:
Wanderlust Worker

Mostly E's:
Healthy Wellness Guru

Mostly A's and E's:
Quiet Retreater

Combination:
Family-Focused Dream

Homesteader's Haven

Summary

You value simplicity and find joy in creating a cozy, grounded life. Your dream is to cultivate a self-sufficient lifestyle surrounded by nature, family, and peace. You believe in working with your hands, growing your own food, and putting love into everything you build.

Advice for Your Dream Life:

- Focus on saving for property or a home that supports your homesteading dreams.
- Invest in tools, classes, or resources that help you learn sustainable living skills.
- Budget for occasional indulgences that enrich your lifestyle, like gardening supplies or farmhouse decor.
- Remember to prioritize balance–you deserve time for rest and play, too!

Glamorous Goal-Digger

Summary

You thrive on ambition and love a life filled with elegance, sophistication, and high achievements. You dream of living in a sleek, modern home, driving a luxury car, and enjoying the finer things in life–all while building a career or business that reflects your brilliance.

Advice for Your Dream Life:

- Set clear financial goals for achieving your luxury lifestyle without sacrificing long-term stability.
- Build a plan for investing and growing your wealth to sustainably fund your dreams.
- Treat yourself to occasional splurges–but make sure they align with your bigger picture.
- Stay grounded and find joy in smaller moments to avoid burnout.

Legacy Builder

Summary

Your heart beats for others, and you dream of leaving an impact on the world. You want a life where you can support your community, give back in meaningful ways, and inspire others to do the same. You find fulfillment in helping others thrive and building a legacy that lasts.

Advice for Your Dream Life:

- Prioritize saving and investing so you can fund your philanthropic efforts.
- Explore financial strategies for charitable giving, like donor-advised funds or scholarships.
- Set boundaries to avoid burnout—your energy is just as important as your impact.
- Don't be afraid to celebrate your successes; you deserve to enjoy the journey!

Wanderlust Worker

Summary

You're all about exploration, adventure, and freedom. Your dream is to travel the world, discover new cultures, and live a life untethered by a traditional career or routines. Experiences mean more to you than possessions, and you thrive on the thrill of the unknown.

Advice for Your Dream Life:

- Create a travel fund and prioritize saving for experiences over material things.
- Consider a career or side hustles that allow remote work or frequent travel.
- Invest in travel-friendly financial tools, like international credit cards or budget-friendly flight services.
- Remember to enjoy the present and make meaningful connections wherever you go.

Healthy Wellness Guru

Summary

Balance and well-being are your top priorities. Your dream life includes plenty of time to focus on your physical, emotional, and spiritual health. You want a peaceful, minimalist lifestyle where you can thrive without unnecessary stress or clutter.

Advice for Your Dream Life:

- Budget for health and wellness expenses, like gym memberships or organic groceries.
- Invest in experiences that align with your self-care goals, like retreats or wellness workshops.
- Use automation to simplify your finances so you can focus on what matters most.
- Set aside time and resources to enjoy life's little luxuries—balance is key!

Quiet Retreater

Summary

You're drawn to quiet moments and meaningful connections. Your dream life revolves around a harmonious blend of solitude and community, living in a cozy space you can call your sanctuary. You value simplicity, peace, and the joy of meaningful relationships.

Advice for Your Dream Life:

- Save for a home or lifestyle that emphasizes comfort and tranquility.
- Build a budget that allows for intentional spending on family, friends, and personal joys.
- Set aside funds to explore hobbies that bring you peace, like reading, painting, or gardening.
- Don't forget to occasionally step out of your comfort zone—you might find joy in unexpected adventures!

Family-Focused Dream

Summary

Your dream life is all about creating a loving, secure environment for you and your family. You prioritize connection, tradition, and making memories with your loved ones. You want to build a legacy of love and stability.

Advice for Your Dream Life:

- Focus on saving for family needs, like education, vacations, and home improvements.
- Create a family budget that includes fun activities and moments of togetherness.
- Invest in experiences that strengthen your bond, like family trips or shared hobbies.
- Remember to carve out time for your own growth and self-care—it will turn you into an even stronger support system!

“It’s about creating a life that feels good for you”

Goal Setting Blueprint

Hey, beautiful soul.

Let's take a moment to put your dreams into action, shall we? I know life can get crazy sometimes–full of distractions, responsibilities, and doubts that whisper, "You're not _________ enough". But guess what? You're here, which means you've already taken a big step toward something extraordinary!

You know those dreams you wrote down earlier? The ones you've been putting off because they feel too big, too scary, or maybe too far out of reach? They're not random. They've been placed on your heart for a reason. They're waiting for you to show up and own them.

The time is now to take those dreams seriously. Not next year. Not when everything feels perfect.

Right. Now.

Because here's the truth: waiting for the 'perfect moment' is like a farmer who waits for the perfect weather to plant her seeds–she never plants, and so she is never able to harvest ... not even a few of her crops. She completely misses all the opportunities by waiting in fear and doubt. Life doesn't wait for us, so we shouldn't wait for life's circumstances. The conditions will never be perfect, but here's the beautiful part: the act of starting creates its own vision. What feels uncertain or overwhelming right now will become manageable over time as you move forward.

However, the only way the farmer can grow her crop is to plant her first seed today.

You've got this. Now let's make it happen!

1. Identify Two Goals

Here's the plan:

We're keeping it simple and focused. Choose two goals—big or small, it doesn't matter. What matters is that they mean something to you.

Maybe it's something you've been putting off because it feels intimidating. Maybe it's a dream you've been too scared to say out loud. Or maybe it's just something practical that will make your life a little easier. Whatever it is, **write it down.** This is your safe space to own it and claim it as yours.

2. Break It Down Into Steps

Big dreams can feel overwhelming, but they're really just a series of small steps. Break each of your goals down into action steps. Think of these steps as all the ingredients you need to make your cake (with no substitutions, of course).

Write down each step, no matter how small, and focus on checking them off one by one. With each checkmark, you're proving to yourself that you've got what it takes to make this happen.

3. Celebrate Your Wins

Now this is our favorite part: once you've completed your goal(s), celebrate them! Pick a reward for yourself–something that feels exciting, meaningful, or just downright fun!

Oath to Self:

The "Aligned with My Values" Oath

I commit to aligning my spending with my core values and dreams. Every financial choice I make will reflect what truly matters to me and the vision I have for my life. I will:

Focus on building a life that feels truly authentic, meaningful, and aligned with my dreams—not one dictated by society's expectations or trends.

Prioritize intentionality over impulse, ensuring that every dollar spent contributes to the future I'm working toward (or the type of rest I prefer).

Embrace challenges, sacrifices, and discipline as stepping stones to financial freedom and peace.

Celebrate my wins, big and small, as proof that I am capable of achieving them all.

I release the need for perfection and comparison. Instead, I promise to honor my unique journey, trusting that each step I take brings me closer to the life I've dreamed of. My money tells the story of who I am and what I stand for—and I choose to make it an inspiring one.

____

Sign here

Section 4:

Appreciating What You Have & Using It

Appreciate How Far You've Come

The best way to go far is to start by appreciating where you are. Like, seriously, take a moment to reflect on how far you've already come, then take a look back to your starting line.

- What choices (sacrifices) have you made? How have they paid off?
- What's one thing you love about your current situation that you used to take for granted?
- How have your values or priorities evolved over time?

Celebrate the seemingly little steps you've taken. If you don't, you'll lose fuel before you even get to the big steps. When you focus on moving quickly (or leaping ahead) instead of walking steadily, you will lose pieces of your self-esteem and motivation. Just imagine how much farther you can go by slowing down and enjoying your journey! When you walk, you can enjoy the sights and process smoothly. However, when you leap, you're only worried about how much energy you have to keep on leaping. Slow down, smell the flowers, and appreciate what you already have. Gratitude is fuel for your hiking journey. Without it, you'll always be chasing the next thing, forgetting the progress you've already made.

Reflecting on What You Have

Once you've taken the time to appreciate where you are, let's figure out what you already have to help you get even further. What tools or resources are available to you? These don't have to be tangible things like money or equipment—maybe it's a skill you've mastered, your best friend who's really good at constructive criticism, or even lessons you learned the hard way. You've got tools, trust me. You might even be surprised by how much you've got going for you.

Take a moment to sit with this question:

What do I already have to help me reach my goals?

Write it down, sis. No, seriously—grab a pen. Define your tangible tools as well as your intangible ones.

Once you've got that list, let's flip it into action:

How can I use what I have to help me along the way?

See? You're already winning without even realizing it! And okay, maybe you don't have everything just yet—that's cool. But don't sleep on the fact that you've got a solid foundation.

Now, let's figure out what's missing so you can fill in the gaps:

What else do I need to reach my goals?

This little exercise is a game-changer. Writing it all down makes it real and shows you how far you've come. Take a second to hype yourself up. You're killing it, and you deserve to feel great about where you are. Go ahead & prove that to yourself by celebrating tonight (in your own way of course)!

Preparing for the Hike Ahead

Alright, now that you've got your starting lineup, let's talk strategy. You've got strengths and weaknesses, just like everyone else. But here's a little secret: your strengths may cover for your weak spots if you play it smart. Let's quickly talk about them. What are the strengths and weaknesses that might shape your journey? This reflection will help you to prepare better for challenges and leverage your unique abilities.

Strengths:

Weaknesses:

How will you prepare yourself for stumps along the way? For example, if you're messy but great at planning, create a system that works for you. There's no shame–just solutions. Be honest with yourself and take the time to craft solutions that will work for you. **Do some research by scrolling on social media, using search engines or AI, or even talking to your friends.**

How can I prepare for potential roadblocks along the way?

Understand that this will only lift some of the load for you, however, you must continue to endure your hike.

Wordplay Activity

"The Month I Gave Up Shopping: A Tale of ________(Adjective) Resilience"

Once upon a time, in the ________________(**adjective**) town of ________________________(**made-up place name**), lived a woman named __________________(**name**). One day, she decided to stop shopping for an entire month. "It'll be _________________(**adjective**)," she said confidently, holding her _____________ (**object**). Little did she know, she was about to embark on a journey of __________________(**adjective**) resourcefulness and _________________________(**adjective**) substitutions.

On Day 1, she realized she was out of _______________(**common household item**). "No worries," she said, "I'll just use ____________(**random object**) instead. It's practically the same thing!" Spoiler alert: it was not.

By Day 5, she ran out of shampoo. With no ______________(**liquid**) in sight, she decided to mix ____________ (**ingredient**) and ______________(**ingredient**) to create her own. "______________________(**exclamation**)!" she cried after trying it. "I smell like ______________________(**scent**)!"

Day 10 brought new challenges. She was craving ______________________(**favorite meal**), but didn't have _________________(**key ingredient**). Instead, she substituted _________________(**random food item**) for it. "It's like ____________________(**celebrity chef name**) always says," she mused, "____(**funny cooking advice**)." The result tasted like ____________________(**adjective**) _____________________(**noun**), but she ate it anyway.

By Day 15, she ran out of toothpaste. "No problem," she said, confidently mixing ________________(**substance**) and ________________(**another substance**). As she brushed, she couldn't help but think, "My teeth feel so ________________ (**adjective**). Is this what ________________________(**famous character**) would use?"

Her wardrobe also took a hit. When her favorite __________(**article of clothing**) ripped, she patched it with ______________(**random object**). "Call me ____________(**superhero name**), because I'm saving the day!" she declared, strutting around like she was on a __________________(**type of event**).

By Day 20, she was talking to her ________________(**pet or plant**) about her journey. "Do you think I'll make it?" she asked. They responded with a ___________________________(**funny response**).

On Day 25, she faced her ultimate challenge: running out of dish detergent. "___________________________(**exclamation**)!" she exclaimed, looking at her pile of dirty dishes. She ended up washing them with ____________________(**random liquid**) while humming ____________________________(**catchy song**).

Finally, Day 30 arrived. She stood in her _________________(**place in home**), looked around at her ___________(**adjective**) creations and whispered, "I did it. I am the ___________ _______(**noun**) of budgeting." She felt _______________(**emotion**), _______________(**emotion**), and a little bit ________________(**adjective**).

As she walked to the store for the first time in a month, she smiled. Next time, I'm giving up _________________(**ridiculous thing**) instead, she thought.

THE END.

The "No Grocery Store Run" Challenge

How It Works

For one week, challenge yourself to make meals only with ingredients you already have at home.

Extra Hard Version: No repeating the same dish twice.

Affirmations to Reflect On During the Challenge:

- Gratitude fuels my heart, even in difficult times. There is always something to appreciate.
- Happiness doesn't have to be grand. I can find it in the simple, ordinary moments.
- Gratitude is my superpower. It transforms my perspective and my life.

1. What are you proud of that you've done so far? How have your values or priorities evolved over time?

2. What's one thing you love about your current situation that you used to take for granted?

3. Do you have solid strategies for your "roadblocks"?

If not, take time to research your roadblocks. Understand them, so you can crush through them. Use AI if you have to because this is a very important step in changing your mindset. Because what happens when you're unprepared and fall on your hike? You bust up your knees and decide you're only going to go so much further. Not over here sis, we're finishing this hike.

"The best way to go far is by
appreciating where you are."

Financial Personality Quiz

What's Your Money Mindset Trigger?

This quiz will help you uncover your financial personality and the triggers that may be influencing your weaknesses. Choose the answer that feels most like you.

1. When I think about budgeting, my first reaction is...

A. "It's too restrictive. I just want to live!"
B. "It's essential. I need to know where every penny goes."
C. "I'll get to it later. It's not urgent right now."
D. "I'm not sure where to start. It feels overwhelming."

2. When I splurge on something, I usually feel...

A. Thrilled–but only in the moment.
B. Like I've failed–I should've saved that money.
C. Indifferent–it doesn't seem like a big deal.
D. Nervous–I'm unsure if I made the right choice.

3. My financial goals are...

A. A little vague–I don't want to be tied down.
B. Detailed and ambitious–I've planned them carefully.
C. Something I know I should have, but I procrastinate.
D. Intimidating–I don't know how to achieve them.

4. When I think about saving for the future, I feel...

A. Conflicted–shouldn't I enjoy life now?
B. Responsible–it's the smart thing to do.
C. Disconnected–it's hard to prioritize something so far away.
D. Overwhelmed–it's hard to know how much is enough.

5. I tend to overspend when...

A. I'm out with friends or feeling bored.
B. I've been sticking to a strict budget for too long.
C. I don't realize how much I've been spending.
D. I'm feeling stressed or uncertain.

6. The thought of tracking my spending feels...

A. Restrictive—I don't want to obsess over every dollar.
B. Natural—it's just part of managing money.
C. Like a hassle—it's not something I think about often.
D. Confusing—I don't even know where to start.

7. If I get an unexpected lump sum, I'm most likely to...

A. Treat myself to something fun or exciting.
B. Put it all into savings.
C. Let it sit in my account without a plan.
D. Worry about how to best use it.

8. I struggle with money when...

A. I feel pressured to keep up with others.
B. I feel like I'm not making progress fast enough.
C. I ignore small habits that add up over time.
D. I feel paralyzed and overthink every decision.

8. When it comes to investing, I feel...

A. Intimidated—it seems too risky.
B. Excited—I love the idea of growing my money.
C. Indifferent—I'll figure it out someday.
D. Anxious—I don't fully understand how it works.

5. My financial decisions are most influenced by...

A. My emotions and the desire to enjoy the moment.
B. My need to stick to a plan and feel in control.
C. My tendency to avoid money conversations or decisions.
D. My fear of making the wrong move.

Results: Your Financial Personality

If you chose mostly A's:

The Free Spirit

Trigger:

FOMO (Fear of Missing Out). You struggle with balancing living in the moment with preparing for the future.

Tip

Set a fun allowance so you can spend guilt-free while staying on track. Take that money out in cash so you don't overspend.

If you chose mostly B's:

The Planner

Trigger:

Perfectionism. You may get stuck in the idea that everything needs to go exactly as planned, leading to burnout or frustration.

Tip

Build flexibility into your plan to allow room for spontaneity and joy. It doesn't have to be a lot, but you need to have fun with your money. You're not only saving for stability, but also freedom!

If you chose mostly C's:

The Procrastinator

Trigger:

Avoidance. You might delay decisions, thinking things will sort themselves out later.

Tip

Start small. Pick one financial habit to work on today, like tracking your spending or automating your savings. Put your bills on autopay & try smart investing tactics like auto-investing.

If you chose mostly D's:

The Overthinker

Trigger:

Analysis paralysis. You spend so much time trying to make the perfect choice you end up feeling stuck.

Tip

Focus on progress, not perfection. Take one step forward and refine as you go. Usually with money moves, if you change your mind, you can always make another move. Don't be afraid of making the wrong decision. Nothing's set in stone!

The "No Comparison Game" Oath

I vow to stop comparing my life,
my finances, and my journey to anyone else's.
I will honor the uniqueness of my path,
understanding that my goals, dreams, and
timeline are mine alone.
I will resist the pressure to chase what society
defines as success, knowing that true success
is living a life aligned with my own values.

I promise to celebrate my progress, no matter how small, and to appreciate the resources, strengths, and opportunities I already have. I will focus on building a life that reflects my priorities, not the standard norm.

I will embrace gratitude as my compass and authenticity as my guide. From this day forward, my money will reflect my vision, my purpose, and the dreams I am working toward–not someone else's version of happiness.

I release the need to compare,
and I choose to celebrate my own journey,
one step at a time.

____

Sign here

Section 5:

Stewarding Your Money Well

Alright, love, it's time to get down to the nitty gritty. You're doing your best, but sometimes "your best" might feel like it's not enough with doing your budget. You've **mostly** got things under control, but deep down, you know you could be doing better. That's okay—we're here to get this money thing on lock **together**. You're not alone in this, and we know you've got what it takes to take full control of your money. Believe in yourself like we believe in you.

The first thing you have to understand is that you need a budget template or tracker. I know, I know—ugh, spreadsheets. But hear me out! You need to clearly see your money all in one place. Do a little research and take some time to find one that you like. Or you can head over to wisemindsshop.org for our budget template. You do not have to use ours, however let us explain a budget to you.

In every standard budget, one should see their income, expenses, and outstanding debt.

That's all you really need.

Income: Any money coming in (or staying in your account).

Expenses: Any money going out (mostly bills).

Outstanding Debt: Anything you owe that you can't pay back right away.

Once you have your budget all in one place and can see the whole picture, you'll be able to compare your totals. In comparing numbers side by side, you can see if you're spending too much—and what you're spending it on. It might be a little messy at first, but we're not here to judge, okay? We're here to grow.

Progress, girlfriend!

So how do you operate this budget? We'll be honest... we can't just give you a simple numerical ratio to follow because everyone's situation is so different. However, here's a few step-by-step instructions for you to help:

1. **Pay your bills first:** (including yourself! Don't skip this part of Step 1)
2. **Cover what's necessary right now** -groceries, gas, and necessities.
3. **What about everything else?** Do what you can with what's left (i.e. additional savings, paying off additional debt, or having fun).

Life isn't perfect, and your monthly budget won't be either. Some months, you're gonna kill it—you'll use less than 20% of your credit card's balance and pay yourself $600. Other months, it'll feel like survival mode; you may only be able to save just a few bucks. That's okay! Do what you can in the moment.

The goal is progress, not perfection.

Budgeting
is mantaining

Money

Name	Type	Balance	After bills
	Checking		
	Savings		
	Short Term Savings Total:		
	Roth IRA		
	Long Term Savings Total:		
	Total:		

*After Bills = Checking - Bills this Period - Debt amount I can afford to pay off

$ "Believe in yourself like we believe in you." $

Bills

Income : $

Name	Paid from?	Date	Amount	Paid?
Rent	Checking			
Self-Care				

Total Bills This Period

*Always round up with bills to avoid overdraft or poor planning (i.e. impulsive spending)

$ "We're here to grow." $

Credit Cards & Loans

# of Cards	Bank Name	Card Name	Statement Date	Interest Rate	Limit
					$10,000
Total:					

# of Loans	Bank Name	Loan Type	Due Date	Monthly Payment	Balance
Total:					

Amount I can afford to pay off this pay period:

Balance	Usuage Rate	Keep Under %	Keep Under Limit	Pay Off Amount
$2,800	28%	20%	$2000	$800

"Budgeting is maintaining"

Money

Name	Type	Balance	After bills
	Checking		
	Savings		
	Short Term Savings Total:		
	Roth IRA		
	Long Term Savings Total:		
	Total:		

*After Bills = Checking - Bills this Period - Debt amount I can afford to pay off

$ "Believe in yourself like we believe in you." $

Bills

Income: $

Name	Paid from?	Date	Amount	Paid?
Rent	Checking			
Self-Care				

Total Bills This Period

*Always round up with bills to avoid overdraft or poor planning (i.e. impulsive spending)

$ "We're here to grow." $

Credit Cards & Loans

# of Cards	Bank Name	Card Name	Statement Date	Interest Rate	Limit
					$10,000
Total:					

# of Loans	Bank Name	Loan Type	Due Date	Monthly Payment	Balance
Total:					

Amount I can afford to pay off this pay period:

Balance	Usage Rate	Keep Under %	Keep Under Limit	Pay Off Amount
$2,800	28%	20%	$2000	$800

$ "Budgeting is maintaining" $

After you track and budget for this pay period,

let's pause and reflect:

- **How do I feel about my money right now?**

○ Scared
○ Confident
○ Ehh, okay, I guess
○ Something else: ____________________

- **What can I cut back on?**

○ Subscriptions I barely use
○ Eating out (do we really need all those DoorDash runs?)
○ Spoiling my kids or fur babies
○ Other:___________________________

- **Where did I spend too much money?**

○ Habit shopping or unnecessary splurges
○ Bills that could be negotiated down
○ Other:___________________________

- How much more can I realistically save each pay period without stretching my wallet?

Between

$______________ and $______________.

- Do I need to make more money to survive,

or

do I just want more to feel comfortable?

(circle one)

Okay now, take a few deep breaths. Sit with this for a second.
Is it as bad as you thought? Probably not. You're most likely doing just fine. You just need a few tweaks, that's all!

If saving is an option for you right now, let's make it automatic and start protecting that long-term money. Set up a recurring transfer to your savings account—your bank's website or app can help you do this in minutes. Treat it like a non-negotiable bill, because it is, girlfriend. Make the amount something you can achieve consistently, even in your tightest months. You can always adjust it later, but right now, the key is strengthening this habit and making sure you get paid on time.

If saving isn't an option for you right now, that's okay—take another deep breath. Let's shift gears and look at ways you can bring in more money. Finding a better-paying job is always a great goal, but let's be real—it's not an overnight fix. So, let's focus on what you can do right now. What skills or talents do you already have that could bring in some extra cash?

Are you an animal lover? Try working through dog-walking or pet-sitting apps—it's a great way to get some fresh air and make money at the same time. Are you talented at doing makeup, nails, or hair? Offer your services to busy moms, especially dance moms—they're always looking for someone who can make their kids shine on stage. Are you an artist or creative soul? Sell your creations online or at local events, and make sure to market yourself on social media platforms.

It might start small... and that's totally fine. Over time, your side hustle could grow into something bigger—it could even become your main source of income. Remember, love, this isn't just about making money—it's about taking control of your life!

Let's do this intentionally and take the first step today.

The "Round-Up Savings" Game

How It Works

For every purchase you make over the course of a week, round up to the nearest $1 or $5, and put the difference into savings. For example, if you spend $12.30, save $2.70 (to round up to $15). **There are apps available that will do this for you automatically.**

Extra Hard Version: Round up to the nearest $10. If you spend $12.30, save $7.70 (to round up to $20).

Why It's Fun

- It feels like a scavenger hunt for spare change.
- Adds an element of surprise to savings—you'll be amazed at how quickly small amounts add up.

Affirmations to Reflect On During The Challenge:

- Maintaining my budget = maintaining my life.
- I am able to save for my future and recognize the power of consistency.
- I protect my financial boundaries and say no to what doesn't serve my goals.

Wordplay Activity
My Bank Account's Dream Speech

"Tonight, we honor the incredible journey of ____________(**your name**)! This award is for their hard work, determination, and finally giving me _______________(**the bank account**) the love I've always deserved.

I remember when your savings account was well below _______________(**number**) dollars. But now? I'm sitting pretty at a luxurious _________________(**number**) dollars! You've made smart moves like cutting back on _____________(**splurge item**) and saying yes to ______________________(**saving strategy**). Oh, and can we talk about the time you saved _____________(**dollar amount**) just by ______________________ (**fun savings hack**)? Genius!

Thanks to you, I'm no longer the overdrawn, ______________(**negative emotion**)-filled account of the past. Instead, I'm proud to fund your dreams, like your upcoming trip to _______________(**dream vacation destination**) and that new ________________(**big purchase you're saving for**).

Let's toast to more _________________________(**positive financial habit**) and less ___________________ (**financial bad habit**). I couldn't be prouder of you if I tried!"

"Believe in yourself"

1. What is one thing you're proud of when it comes to how you manage your finances?

2. What are your biggest financial priorities right now?

3. If you were advising a friend in your situation, what encouragement or advice would you give them?

Budgeting Bingo

How It Works

You know what to do. Cover 5 squares vertically, horizontally, or diagonally to win!

Extra Hard Version: Cover 2 sets of 5 squares (or a total of 9 if your bingo lines cross) to win.

Why It's Fun

- It makes budgeting fun and engaging!

B	I	N	G	O
Make a grocery list	Cancel one unused subscription service	Pack a lunch instead of eating out	Visit a farmer's market	Dollar Tree run
DIY a coffee drink at home instead of going through the drive-thru	Find a free entertainment option for the weekend	Style your clothes in a new way (or the wrong way)	Paint your nails yourself instead of going to the salon	Save $____________
Sell one item you no longer need	Plan a "no-spend" day and stick to it	★	Thrifting adventure instead of Marshall's run	Host a potluck instead of going out with friends
Find and download a free budgeting app or template	Add to your savings account daily for one week	Unsubscribe from marketing emails	Put $15 in an envelope labeled "Future Me's Treat."	DIY something instead of buying it
Block a major retailer you see consistently on your feed	Open a savings account through a promotional deal	Go for a local hike around your neighborhood	Write down one positive thing about your financial journey	Donate any amount to a small, yet impactful cause

The "Balanced Stewardship" Oath

"I promise to take charge of my money with both care and intention, knowing that balance is the key to thriving. I will stop making excuses for not saving –my future self deserves a solid foundation, and I have the power to build it. No more procrastinating or telling myself, 'I'll start tomorrow.' Today is the day I choose to plant seeds for my tree to grow.

At the same time, I release the guilt of spending money on things that bring me joy. Life is meant to be lived, and I deserve to celebrate the moments that make my heart full. Whether it's a spontaneous trip, a night out with loved ones, or an item that I've been eyeing for months, I will spend with purpose and intention, knowing that joy is just as valuable as security.

I refuse to let fear or shame control my financial decisions. I will give every dollar I earn a purpose –whether it's saving, investing, or spending. My money is a reflection of what matters to me –not what society, my friends, or social media tells me I should do.

I will hold myself accountable, but I will also show myself grace. If I make a mistake, I won't let it define me. Instead, I'll learn, adjust, and keep moving forward. Period, no excuses.

I choose to see money as a tool–not an obstacle, not a source of stress, but a resource I can manage wisely. I will steward it with care, while balancing between preparing for the future and enjoying the present. My financial journey is mine alone, and I will own every step with confidence, discipline, and a spirit of gratitude."

____

Sign here

Section 6:

What to Do If (and When)

If you've ever been hiking, you know that you'll trip and fall at least one time (or a few if you're a clumsy one) along the way. Well, besties, life's the same way: full of trip-ups. And reaching your financial goals is no different. You know that at some point, you're going to 'trip over a rock'. It's inevitable. But in knowing that you will mess up at some point, how do you prepare yourself for it? How do you position yourself to protect yourself when you trip and fall?

The answer? **You prepare in advance.** You don't just cross your fingers and hope for the best. That's like giving the universe full authority over your life without direction.

So how do you prepare in advance? You throw on some gloves (metaphorically speaking) and set yourself up to bounce back. When it comes to your finances, this means recognizing your weak spots and cushioning those areas before things get messy. It's not about being perfect; it's about planning for the moments where you might make a little oopsie.

We all have financial tendencies that can trip us up. Maybe you're a **spender** who loves to live in the moment, or maybe you're a **saver** who's so locked in on the future that you forget to enjoy today. Neither extreme is healthy—you need balance, sis.

Spenders vs. Savers:
Which One are You?

Spenders

Are all about the here and now. They're the ones saying, "You only live once!" while swiping their cards for the latest gadget, a round of drinks, or whatever catches their eye. The present is their playground; they don't hold back.

Savers

On the other hand, are all about the long game. They sacrifice today's joys for next year's dreams, stashing money away like squirrels hoarding acorns. They live for their ideal future, but sometimes they forget to live in the present.

Most of us lean one way or the other at different points in our lives. But here's the kicker: both ends of the spectrum are toxic. Spenders might wake up one day with empty wallets and regret, while savers could look back and realize they missed out on a lot of life's joys.

The goal isn't to be one or the other—it's to find a happy medium.

Are you currently more of a spender or a saver? You may already know, but take this quiz to make sure.

After you finish, we'll have some advice for you.

Money Personality Quiz:
Are You a Saver or Spender?

1. When you receive an unexpected bonus or gift money, what's your first thought?

A) "How much of this can I save for future goals?"

B) "This is perfect! I've been wanting to treat myself to something!"

2. If you're shopping and see an item you love but don't need, what do you do?

A) Walk away and think about whether it fits your budget and goals.

B) Buy it–you deserve nice things, and you'll figure out the budget later.

3. How do you usually approach budgeting?

A) I track my expenses carefully and stick to a plan.

B) I prefer to go with the flow and spend as needed.

4. What's your attitude toward sales and discounts?

A) I only buy things on sale if they were already in my plan or budget.

B) Sales are exciting–I love scoring a good deal on something fun or useful!

5. When planning a vacation, what's your priority?

A) Finding ways to maximize enjoyment while staying within budget.

B) Making sure I have a luxurious and memorable experience, even if it costs more.

6. How do you feel about credit cards?

A) They're a tool for convenience, but I always pay them off in full.

B) They're great for flexibility, and I'll manage the balance over time.

7. What's your reaction to a financial emergency, like a car repair?

A) I'm grateful I have savings to cover it.

B) I'll figure out a way to pay for it–probably with credit or borrowing.

8. When you set financial goals, how do you approach them?

A) I break them into actionable steps and stick to the plan.

B) I set goals, but tend to prioritize the present moment over strict plans.

9. How do you handle meals or entertainment with friends?

A) I prefer low-cost or home-based activities to keep expenses down.

B) I enjoy going out, even if it means spending more.

10. What's your long-term vision for your money?

A) Building financial security and stability for myself and my family.

B) Living fully in the present while still hoping to reach my goals someday.

Final Results:

Take the # of A's you have & divide by 10 (Saver %). Do the same thing with the # of B's you have (Spender %).

Now you know that you're ____% Saver and ____% Spender.

How to Cushion the Fall

Once you've figured out where you land, it's time to set up those financial "cushions".
Here's some suggestions:

For Spenders:

If you're a "live in the moment" type, try:

- **Locking Up Your Savings in a CD (Certificate of Deposit):** It's like putting your money in a safe with a timer—you can't touch it until it's time. This keeps you from blowing through your savings on impulse buys.
- **Using Cash-Only Spending Limits:** Withdraw a set amount of cash each week for non-essential expenses. When the cash runs out, you're done spending—no swiping allowed!
- **Embrace the "One In, One Out" Rule:** For every new purchase (like clothing or gadgets), commit to selling or donating an item. This not only curbs unnecessary spending, but also keeps your home clutter-free.

Write Your Own:

For Savers:

If you're all about the future and forget to enjoy the now:

- **Create a Fun Fund:** Use your "fun fund" to create memories, like a weekend getaway or a fancy dinner with friends. Think of it as an investment in your well-being. You can even open a separate account specifically for this fund. Attach it to a debit card and pick one day a month where you can swipe impulsively.

- **Ease into Risk-Taking:** Explore low-risk investments or experiences that allow you to step out of your financial comfort zone. For example, invest in yourself through an online course, skill-based class or networking event.

- **Mix Practicality with Pleasure:** Pair necessary expenses with enjoyable experiences. For instance, turn grocery shopping into a fun outing by trying a new café nearby beforehand. This helps you balance necessities with living in the moment.

Create one yourself:

The "**Aim Training**" Game

How It Works

1. Think about a common feeling or trigger that throws you off track when it comes to managing your money (e.g., impulsive spending, fear of scarcity, or guilt over splurging).

2. Create a "clip of ammo" by listing **6-8 techniques, strategies, or affirmations** that can help you combat that feeling or trigger. These could include:
Techniques: "Wait 24 hours before making any large purchases."
Affirmations: "I am in control of my financial decisions."

3. When you feel that trigger or emotion creeping up, "fire off" one of your pieces of ammo to take it down and regain control.

Extra Hard Version: Repeat the process for another trigger or emotion that challenges you. Build a second clip with new, tailored strategies or affirmations.

Why It's Fun

- **Creative Brainstorming:** Coming up with "ammo" allows you to tap into your creativity and problem-solving skills.
- **Confidence Booster:** Every time you "fire off" an affirmation or strategy, you're training yourself to respond positively in tough moments.
- **Progress Tracking:** Watching yourself get better at "hitting the target" is satisfying and encourages continued growth.
- **Empowering Mindset Shift:** This game reframes triggers as opportunities to strengthen your financial habits.

Affirmation to Reflect On During The Challenge:

Thoughts & feelings will come and go, but I am in control of what stays.

Wordplay Activity

The Tale of the Fearless Financial Fighter

Fill in the blanks below to complete the story of a legendary money-slaying hero!

Once upon a time, in the bustling land of _______________(**made-up land name**), there lived a fearless financial fighter named _____________(**your name**). She was known far and wide for her ability to ______________(**empowering verb**) debt and _______________(**positive action**) her financial goals.

Her greatest challenge came in the form of _________________(**scary debt name**), a monstrous financial dragon with claws made of _______________(**expensive item**) and a roar louder than ____________ (**loud object**). Armed with her trusty _______________(**financial tool**) and her shield of _____________________________(**clip of ammo**), she faced the beast head-on.

The battle raged for ____(**number**) months. Though she slashed away at interest rates and dodged unexpected expenses, one particularly sharp ________________(**surprise expense**) knocked her down, leaving her account as empty as ______________(**noun or phrase**).

Defeated but not discouraged, she retreated to her financial sanctuary in ______________(**cozy place**) to regroup. While there, she reflected on her journey, sipping on ______________(**favorite drink**) and strategizing her comeback. "What went wrong?" she asked herself. She practiced ______________________ (**money-saving skill**) and reread her favorite financial wisdom from _______________(**financial guru**), remembering how she once conquered ________________________________(**money challenge or goal**).

After ____(**number**) weeks of planning and persistence, she emerged with a new financial battle plan: __________________(**money strategy**). She charged back into the fight, slaying _______________ (**scary debt name**) with precision and determination, while also saving money in the process!

Victorious, she returned to her community, who greeted her with cheers of _______________(**exclamation**). Her friends admired her not just for her resilience, but for her ability to ______________(**empowering financial verb**) and _______________(**positive action**).

Her legend grew, inspiring others to remember:
"You may stumble, but every stumble is a chance to ____________(**motivational verb**), ____________ (**empowering verb**), and take charge of your financial destiny!"

For Spenders:

1. When do you find yourself most tempted to make unplanned purchases? What usually leads you to say, "I'll just treat myself this one time"?

For Spenders:

2. Are there specific stores, apps, or deals that make you feel like you have to buy something?

For Spenders:

3. How does your screen time affect your ability to focus on financial goals? Does it influence your impulsive spending online?

"Failures do not define me......"

“.......comebacks do!”

For Savers:

1. Are there times when saving feels more like a chore than a choice? Why?

For Savers:

2. How do you decide when it's okay to dip into your savings for something fun?

For Savers:

3. Are your financial decisions driven by a fear of loss or excitement for growth?

The Warrior's Oath to Self

Raise your metaphorical sword
(or your coffee mug) and repeat after me:

I, ____________(Your Name), solemnly swear to embrace my journey as the fearless warrior I am.
I acknowledge that life is a battlefield, full of **high peaks** and **low valleys**, and that every stumble is a chance to learn, grow, and rise stronger than before.

I will not let defeat define me, nor will I allow fear to hold me back.
When challenges arise, I will take a deep breath, steady my shield of resilience, and remember that every dragon I face—whether it's debt, self-doubt, or an unexpected setback—is just another opportunity to prove my strength.

I vow to celebrate my victories, no matter how small.
I know that each step forward is a testament to my determination. When I stumble, I will offer myself grace, understanding that setbacks are simply part of the adventure.

I will stay empowered, even in the face of uncertainty.
I will draw on my courage, creativity, and resourcefulness to keep moving forward. I will choose action over stagnation, reflection over regret, and progress over perfection. ALWAYS.

I promise to honor my dreams, protect my peace, and own my power.
I will not compare my path to others, for my story is uniquely my own. No matter how many times I fall, I will always get back up, ready to take on the next challenge.

I am not just a warrior; I am a legend in the making.
With every step, every choice, and every act of resilience, I am building a legacy of strength, courage, and triumph.

This is my oath, and I will uphold it with pride and love to myself.

____
Sign here

Personality Quiz:

What Type of Financial Warrior Are You?

1. What's your approach to tackling financial challenges?

A) Charge in headfirst and deal with the details later.

B) Carefully analyze the situation before making a move.

C) Create a detailed plan and stick to it, no matter what.

D) Stay calm, steady, and support what I can.

2. When you make a budget, your focus is on:

A) Quick wins–get that immediate payoff!

B) Cutting unnecessary expenses with precision.

C) Building a rock-solid plan for the long term.

D) Covering the essentials and building a strong safety net.

3. How do you react when an unexpected expense comes up?

A) Tackle it right away and adjust later.

B) Take a moment to evaluate my options before deciding.

C) Pull out the emergency plan you've already created.

D) Handle it with patience, relying on savings or resources you've built.

4. What's your financial motto?

A) "Fortune favors the bold!"

B) "Aim small, miss small."

C) "Victory is in the plan."

D) "Slow and steady wins the race."

5. Your ideal financial strategy is:

A) Seizing opportunities as they come.

B) Pinpointing weak spots in your spending.

C) Planning for every possible outcome.

D) Building strong reserves and preparing for the long haul.

6. How do you handle a financial setback?

A) Bounce back quickly and keep moving forward.

B) Evaluate what went wrong and adjust your aim.

C) Reflect, learn, and incorporate this lesson into your strategy.

D) Stay grounded and protect what you've built.

7. What's your biggest financial strength?

A) Your courage to take risks and act quickly.

B) Your sharp eye for unnecessary expenses.

C) Your ability to stay organized and prepared.

D) Your resilience and consistency.

8. If your finances were a weapon, what would they be?

A) A mighty sword–quick, strong, and direct.

B) A bow and arrow–precise and calculated.

C) A battlefield playbook–strategic and well-planned.

D) A shield–solid, reliable, and protective.

9. What's your biggest financial challenge?

A) Slowing down and thinking things through.

B) Trusting your instincts instead of overthinking.

C) Adapting when the plan changes.

D) Taking risks instead of playing it safe.

10. What motivates you to keep fighting for financial freedom?

A) The thrill of achieving big wins.

B) Hitting precise goals you've set for yourself.

C) Knowing that every move brings you closer to victory.

D) The peace of mind that comes with stability.

Results

Mostly A's: The Bold Swordswoman

Description

You're fearless and direct, always ready to tackle financial challenges head-on. Your strength lies in your courage and ability to act quickly, however, don't forget to pause and strategize before charging into battle.

Advice

You're a financial go-getter, seizing opportunities with unwavering courage. Your fearless approach can lead to big wins, but it's important to balance your boldness with foresight. Before charging into financial decisions, take a moment to evaluate the terrain. Planning ahead can protect you from unnecessary losses.

Strengths on the Battlefield:

- Fearless risk-taker: You're not afraid to try new ventures or jump on opportunities.
- Quick action: You don't hesitate, which often gives you a competitive edge.
- Inspires others: Your bold moves encourage those around you to step out of their comfort zone.

Weaknesses on the Battlefield:

- Impulsiveness: Acting too quickly can sometimes lead to missteps.
- Overconfidence: You may underestimate the importance of planning and strategy.
- Vulnerability to burnout: Your high-energy approach could leave you drained if you don't pace yourself.

Mostly B's: The Precise Archer

Description

You're sharp, focused, and detail-oriented, always hitting your financial targets with precision. Just be careful not to get stuck overthinking –sometimes, it's okay to let your arrows fly!

Advice

Your laser focus and ability to pinpoint weaknesses in your financial habits make you a deadly force against wasteful spending. You're great at precision, but sometimes your need for perfection can slow you down. Remember: not every shot has to hit the bullseye. Action, even if it's imperfect, can still lead to progress.

Strengths on the Battlefield:

- Keen eye for detail: You're excellent at spotting opportunities and avoiding waste.
- Calculated decision-making: You don't shoot until you're sure it's the right move.
- Consistent results: Your accuracy leads to steady financial growth.

Weaknesses on the Battlefield:

- Overthinking: You may hesitate and miss chances while waiting for the "perfect moment."
- Limited spontaneity: Your cautious approach can sometimes hold you back from big wins.
- Tunnel vision: Focusing too much on one area may cause you to overlook other opportunities.

Mostly C's: The Strategic Tactician

Description

You're the genius of the battlefield, always three steps ahead. Your plans are legendary, but remember: life doesn't always follow a script. Adaptability is key.

Advice

You're the mastermind behind the scenes, mapping out every step of your financial journey. Your plans are meticulous, but life often throws unexpected curveballs. Learn to embrace flexibility–being able to pivot mid-battle can turn a setback into a surprising victory. Every good plan evolves with the circumstances.

Strengths on the Battlefield:

- Master planner: Your strategies are solid and well thought-out.
- Long-term focus: You excel at building sustainable financial systems.
- Resourceful: You make the most out of every tool and opportunity.

Weaknesses on the Battlefield:

- Rigidity: You may struggle to adapt when plans don't go as expected.
- Over-preparation: Spending too much time planning can delay action.
- Perfectionism: You may avoid risks, fearing failure or imperfection.

Mostly D's: The Steadfast Shieldbearer

Description

You're the protector, steady and reliable in the face of financial challenges. Your strength lies in your resilience and patience, but don't be afraid to take calculated risks to achieve even greater rewards.

Advice

Your patience and resilience make you the fortress of financial stability. You protect what you've built and ensure you're always prepared for the unexpected. However, your cautious nature may prevent you from taking bold steps forward. Don't be afraid to lower your shield and wield your financial resources to achieve your dreams—you're stronger than you think!

Strengths on the Battlefield:

- Resilient: You bounce back from setbacks with unwavering resolve.
- Dependable: You know others can rely on your steady and consistent approach.
- Prepared: Your financial "armor" shields you from unforeseen challenges.

Weaknesses on the Battlefield:

- Risk-averse: You may miss out on big opportunities by playing it too safe.
- Overprotective: Holding onto resources too tightly can limit growth.
- Reluctant to act: Fear of failure can sometimes slow your progress.

Section 7:

The Habitual Practice of Self-Applause

When was the last time you stopped and gave yourself credit? No, seriously. Giving yourself credit, not for hitting the big goals–paying off a loan or reaching your savings target–but for the little moments that got you there, like saying no to that impulse buy or tracking your expenses for the first time in months.

Life isn't about waiting until you've crossed some imaginary finish line to feel proud of yourself. It's about celebrating the moments that prove you're moving forward. Every small win, every lesson learned, every time you choose progress over procrastination–it all matters, girl!

Perfection is overrated anyway. Waiting for things to be perfect before you celebrate is like waiting for it to stop raining before you dance. Honey, dance in that rain! The ups and the downs–they all deserve a little celebration.

Why? Because the journey is where the magic happens! It's where you learn, grow, and transform. Think about it: where were you when you first started this playbook? Before you decided it was time to change? Before you even took this level of interest in your financial well being? You've literally come so far, both in mindset and in money. So, go ahead and do your dance! Recognize that you just did something very challenging. Honey, changing your mindset is **different.** That's another ball game for real, and you better recognize it!

Celebrating your progress doesn't **have** to mean splurging on a big night out (unless you want to). It can be as simple as writing yourself a love note in your journal, indulging in your favorite specialty drink, or giving yourself a well-deserved self-care day. It's about pausing, reflecting, and praising your efforts.

Make this promise to yourself: no more waiting for perfection. No more waiting for the big step. No more saying, "I'm not done yet". Clap because you finished **a step**. Celebrate every movement forward, especially the hard ones. Be proud of your journey and where you are in the moment. Let's choose to honor joy and kick despair out of our mental space because it has no place here. Matter of fact, tell joy to guard the door. Despair does not have a wristband and cannot get in. Despair is banned forever. You are going to continue taking the steps forward to get closer to the life you've been dreaming about.

And that, my friend, is worth celebrating!

Let's get into it!

1. Create a list of small celebrations that you can come back to when it's time to honor joy.

2. Create a list of big celebrations for when you want to downright spoil yourself.

2. What are you most proud of about your journey through this playbook? List your wins (big and small, of course)!

The "Vision Budget" Challenge

How It Works

Instead of a standard budget, create a budget based on your life goals. Allocate any amount of money toward categories like "dream vacation" or "business idea" and automate it to make it easier!

It can be as small as $5 every payday, but you have to fund your dream(s). No take-backsies, your dreams are a non-negotiable.

Why It's Impactful:

- Makes budgeting feel exciting and meaningful rather than restrictive.
- Aligns financial habits with personal values and dreams.
- Keeps you motivated by focusing on what money can do for your future.

Personality Quiz:

What's Your Celebration Anthem?

Find out which iconic celebration song best fits your vibe! Answer these questions and tally up your A's, B's, C's, and D's to discover your ultimate anthem.

1. How do you like to start a celebration?

A. With a big announcement to let everyone know it's time to party!
B. By soaking up good vibes and smiling from ear to ear.
C. I get moving right away—dancing is a must!
D. I hype myself up with a big "Let's go!" moment.

2. How do you feel after a big win?

A. Proud and ready to share the moment with others.
B. Calm and content—it's all about the good vibes.
C. Excited and bursting with energy —I can't contain it!
D. Like an unforgettable night is just starting.

3. What's your ideal party setting?

A. A classic celebration with music, balloons, and lots of people.
B. A sunny outdoor spot where everyone's smiling and relaxed.
C. A modern space with bright lights and a great dance floor.
D. A high-energy party with music pumping all night long.

4. Your go-to dance move at a party is:

A. The timeless two-step—simple but iconic!
B. A carefree sway, letting the music flow through me.
C. Full-on choreography—I'm here to impress!
D. Jumping, fist-pumping, and hyping up the crowd.

5. What's the most important part of a celebration?

A. Bringing people together to share in the joy.
B. Feeling good about yourself and the moment.
C. Moving and grooving to celebrate the win.
D. Making memories you'll be talking about forever.

6. How do you celebrate a personal milestone?

A. With a party that everyone's invited to—it's a big deal!
B. By taking time to appreciate how far I've come.
C. By treating myself to a fun, feel-good experience.
D. By making an entire day unforgettable from start to finish.

7. Your playlist for the perfect party includes:

A. Feel-good classics that everyone knows and loves.
B. Upbeat, positive songs with a message of gratitude.
C. Energetic tracks that make you want to dance instantly.
D. High-energy hits that keep the party thriving.

8. Your celebration outfit is:

A. Bold and festive—it says, "Look at me!"
B. Bright and cheerful—it's all about good vibes.
C. Colorful and fun—it makes me feel alive!
D. Edgy and party-ready—I'm here to have a blast.

9. How do you end a celebration?

A. With a heartfelt toast or thank-you to everyone.
B. By reflecting on how great it felt to share the joy.
C. By dancing until I'm exhausted and smiling all the way home.
D. By yelling, "What a night!" and sharing laughs with friends.

10. How do you make sure the celebration is unforgettable?

A. By creating a warm and inclusive vibe for everyone.
B. By focusing on the happiness the moment brings.
C. By getting everyone up out of their seats to dance.
D. By making it an epic, high-energy event that's nonstop fun.

Your Celebration Anthem Results!

Mostly A's:
"Celebrate" by Kool & The Gang

Your Style:

You're a classic celebrator who loves gathering people to share in the joy. Whether it's a big party or a small gathering, your energy creates an uplifting atmosphere. You believe celebrations are best when shared!

Strengths:

You are warm, inviting, and great at bringing people together.

Watch Out For:

Putting so much effort into others' joy that you forget to enjoy the moment yourself.

Mostly B's:
"Happy" by Pharrell Williams

Your Style:

For you, celebrating is all about the feel-good vibes. You find joy in the little things and know how to savor the happiness of each moment. Your positivity is contagious, and people love being around you.

Strengths:

You are grateful, content, and able to find happiness in any situation.

Watch Out For:

Downplaying your own wins—don't forget that you deserve to shine, too!

Mostly C's:

"Can't Stop the Feeling" by Justin Timberlake

Your Style:

You're all about movement and energy! Celebrating for you means dancing like nobody's watching and spreading joy wherever you go. Your infectious enthusiasm makes every celebration better.

Strengths:

You are energetic, playful, and a natural mood booster.

Watch Out For:

Overcommitting to being the life of the party –take time to recharge, too.

Mostly D's:

"I Gotta Feeling" by The Black Eyed Peas

Your Style:

You're the ultimate hype-person who turns any celebration into an unforgettable event. From start to finish, you bring high energy, good vibes, and excitement to everything you do.

Strengths:

You are dynamic, adventurous, and always up for a good time.

Watch Out For:

Expecting every celebration to be perfect– the simple moments can be just as meaningful.

Wordplay Activity
The Endurance Oath

Fill in the blanks to create a personalized oath to celebrate your progress, stay grounded, and keep moving forward.

I, ______________________(**name**), promise to celebrate every ______________(**adjective**) step I take, whether it's ____________________(**small action**) or ________________________________(**big accomplishment**). I vow to find ________________(**emotion**) in the ________________(**noun**) and to honor every ______________________(**adjective**) milestone along the way.

Instead of _________________(**verb ending in -ing**) forward too fast, I will take steady _______________ (**plural noun**), knowing that __________________(**verb ending in -ing**) my dream(s) will come with consistent & intentional ________________(**plural noun**).

I pledge to _________________(**verb**) where I am today and _________________(**verb**) where I'm going, staying _________________(**adjective**) in my journey. No matter what _________________(**noun**) comes my way, I will ________________(**verb**) my ________________(**adjective**) goals and keep moving toward ________________(**noun**), because I know this is the path to true __________________(**emotion**) and ______________________(**emotion**).

This is my loving promise to myself: to _________________(**verb**) my progress, to ________________(**verb**) my challenges, and to __________________(**verb**) my own unique journey.

____

Sign here

Celebration Wordsearch

A	E	C	F	I	O	E	D	U	T	I	T	A	R	G	U	A	C	J	O	Y
R	G	H	S	N	H	U	W	E	Q	E	N	O	T	S	E	L	I	M	B	G
I	J	O	H	T	W	O	R	G	D	O	U	B	G	I	C	A	H	N	S	U
L	M	I	I	E	F	S	P	C	C	T	K	L	S	T	E	P	S	L	A	P
H	O	C	E	N	I	B	U	O	H	W	S	Q	J	U	L	O	B	U	T	I
P	T	E	S	T	U	S	K	C	A	K	P	E	I	W	E	F	F	O	R	T
E	I	S	J	I	C	Q	A	C	C	J	U	P	R	F	B	O	I	J	W	S
E	V	I	N	O	K	O	F	R	E	E	D	O	M	H	R	S	C	L	I	E
P	A	Q	U	N	S	P	U	R	P	O	S	E	L	E	A	S	T	R	N	C
E	T	Q	H	A	B	I	T	S	S	K	A	S	Y	E	T	I	M	E	S	N
C	I	C	E	L	O	G	O	S	U	I	M	E	P	T	E	N	I	S	I	A
N	O	E	I	T	Y	R	E	S	E	T	N	D	T	E	O	A	N	I	S	D
E	N	S	M	G	N	R	E	T	I	R	O	L	E	C	N	A	D	L	T	N
I	H	I	T	E	G	O	S	I	U	T	A	M	L	A	T	O	S	I	E	U
T	U	A	G	O	O	D	E	O	D	I	C	A	P	I	E	T	E	E	K	B
A	S	R	R	S	L	T	J	S	F	O	R	W	A	R	D	V	T	N	I	A
P	T	P	R	C	O	N	F	I	D	E	N	C	E	S	L	I	S	C	T	F
B	E	S	P	I	E	L	O	R	T	N	O	C	F	L	E	S	N	E	O	C

1. Progress
2. Celebrate
3. Good
4. Times
5. Mindset
6. Joy
7. Growth
8. Success
9. Journey
10. Dance
11. Wins
12. Forward
13. Habits
14. Patience
15. Purpose
16. Effort
17. Intentional
18. Gratitude
19. Resilience
20. Freedom
21. Steps
22. Choices
23. Milestone
24. Praise
25. Confidence
26. Self Control
27. Motivation
28. Abundance
29. Rest
30. Reset

Vision Board Page(s)!

Instructions:

A vision board is your space to visually dream, design, and define your goals! It is a powerful tool that brings your goals to life, so make it personal, creative, and uniquely yours.

Here's how to use this space:

1. Choose Your Method(s):

- **Scrapbook or Junk Journal:** Cut and paste words, images, and colors from magazines or printouts that inspire you and align with your goals.
- **Sketch or Draw:** Create your own visuals—whether it's your dream home, financial milestone, or future accomplishment.
- **Colorize:** Use vibrant colors to represent emotions, progress, and energy behind your goals.

2. Focus on All Areas of Your Life:

Think beyond just money—consider your personal growth, career, and dreams as well. This is about the life you're building.

3. Be Intentional:

Add meaningful quotes or affirmations that resonate with you and inspire action!

Congratulations!

You did it! You've reached the end of The New Self-Care: A Playbook for Money Mindset Reset! Pause for a moment to really let that sink in and give yourself the credit you absolutely deserve. This wasn't just about reading through pages or answering questions. It was about doing something incredible: investing in yourself. You've taken the time to reset your mindset, challenge old habits, and step into a new chapter of your life. That's not just progress—that's transformation—and it's all because of you!

This journey was **not easy.** You've faced tough questions, confronted hard truths, and made decisions that required courage and discipline. But guess what? You kept going and powered through! Every moment of reflection and every step you took toward understanding your money mindset was a testament to your resilience. You **chose** to rewrite the narrative, take control of your life, and build a foundation for your future. And girlfriend, I'm so proud of you.

Do you realize how much you've accomplished?

You didn't just finish a book —you took the first steps toward a better version of yourself! You proved that you're capable of growth, no matter where you started. You've made the effort to move past limiting beliefs, to embrace progress over perfection, and to prioritize yourself and your dreams. That's a really big deal, and something not everyone has the strength or determination to do. You should feel so proud of yourself right now!

As you move forward, keep this momentum going. Keep growing, keep learning, and keep progressing. The steps you've taken over the course of this book will ripple into every part of your life. You've laid a foundation for something truly beautiful—a life where you feel empowered, in control, and confident about the future. So celebrate this moment! Clap for yourself and treat yourself to something special. You've earned it!

Let me tell you something. This is only the beginning of all the amazing things you're capable of. Let this be a reminder to you:

You're unstoppable, you're more than capable and the best is yet to come.

Ideas For How To Celebrate Your Wins

Every accomplishment–big or small–deserves a moment of celebration.

Why?

Because failing to celebrate can rob us of the joy of today. This can lead to deepening our feelings of dissatisfaction, and causing us to miss out on the wonderful beauty of the present. Don't let life's wins–no matter how small–slip by without a little "Hooray!"

Celebrations That Cost Nothing

- **Relax:** Take a soothing bubble bath with candles and music.
- **Cozy Up:** Get comfy for a movie night at home with something new or a personal favorite.
- **Unwind:** Go for a self-care walk & explore your neighborhood or local park.
- **DIY Spa:** Pamper yourself with a facial, mani, or by deep conditioning your hair. We know you already have some of this stuff in your closet!
- **Dance Party:** Charge those headphones, close those curtains, blast your favorite playlist and dance like nobody's watching.
- **Center Yourself:** Meditate on all your wins and progress throughout your life.
- **Be Creative:** Create a scrapbook page (or junk journal). Use what you have at home or can find for free.

Celebrations That Cost Nothing

- **Treat Your Tastebuds:** Cook a special meal (or dessert) with ingredients you already have in your pantry.
- **Indulge Your Hobby:** Dive into reading, painting, or something new.
- **Pause for Beauty:** Watch the sunrise or sunset and reflect. Or do your makeup really cute for no reason at all & pause on your own beauty!
- **Dream Big:** Make a dream vision board—and don't hold back! It doesn't cost anything to dream.
- **Collect Your Wins:** Make yourself a victory jar filled with all your wins. When you need a pick-me-up, you can go back and reflect on each one of them.
- **Write Yourself a Love Letter:** Reflect on how far you've come and all the things you admire about yourself.
- **Stargaze:** Lay under the night sky with a blanket and soak in the beauty of creation.
- **Compliment Sprint:** Spend a day giving genuine compliments to yourself in the mirror and to others around you—it's a mood booster!
- **Declutter Party:** Refresh your space by organizing and/or donating things you no longer need. A clean space is a celebration in itself!

Celebrations That Are Low Cost

- **Sip & Savor:** Treat yourself to a fancy coffee, tea, or glass of wine.
- **Bloom Bright:** Buy yourself a small bouquet of fresh flowers.
- **Indulge:** Enjoy a sweet or savory pastry from your local bakery.
- **Thrift Find:** Hunt for a new treasure at a thrift store or flea market.
- **Escape:** Rent or download a book or movie you've been curious about. Check your local library first to see if they offer any of these services for you.
- **Chef's Kiss:** Experiment with a new recipe you've been dying to try.
- **Mini Luxury:** Grab a travel-sized skincare treat or perfume for pampering yourself.
- **Catch a Flick:** Go to a discounted movie showing (some theaters have discount days or deals within their app).
- **Photoshoot:** Get dressed up with a friend, visit a local art gallery (or library even), and take a few pictures for social media.
- **Splurge a little:** Try that subscription box you've been eyeing for a month (i.e jewelry, hair care, skin care, makeup, sweet treats, etc.)
- **Handmade Jewelry:** Pick up some beads or materials at a craft store and make something you'll love wearing.
- **Local Adventure:** Visit a nearby museum, park, or cultural spot with a small entry fee.

Savings Tips

Budgeting and Planning

1. Automate Your Savings! Schedule automatic transfers to your savings account every payday. Start with something manageable like $50. (You can always pay yourself more after budgeting.)

2. Track Every Expense for 1-3 Months: Use an app & connect all your accounts to see how much of your money is going to expenses, subscriptions, shopping sprees, etc. Use a notebook if you prefer to see it on paper! The ONLY way to fully control your money is to know where it's going.

3. Plan Your Meals Weekly! Meal prepping is the new IT girl trend since it saves you time–but it also saves you money. You don't always have to have your meals prepped in the fridge, but buying ingredients that will be used across meals saves you some hassle. **Example Week: 5-Veggie Spaghetti, Italian Pasta Salad, BLTs, Veggie & Cheese Omlets, Pita Pizza, and Mediterranean Salads.**

4. Pay Yourself First Always: Treat savings as a non-negotiable "bill" you pay alongside everything else. This is why it's important to know your monthly expenses & how much wiggle room you have. Can you afford an extra expense of $200-400 every month? If so, this amount should be added to your monthly bills.

5. Do a "No-Spend Day" Each Week: Dedicate one day where you don't spend any money at all (hard version: see how many days you can keep up with this!) Try to make it a habit to spend money intentionally. If shopping is your "dopamine hit", replace this habit with something healthy like revamping your clothes or styling them differently.

6. Focus on High-Interest Debt First: Make extra payments on high-interest loans or credit cards to save on interest costs. It doesn't matter if it's a double payment or a few extra dollars, it's helping you save on interest in the long run.

7. Take Advantage of Employer Matches: If your job offers a 401(k) match, make it a priority to invest something–that's essentially free money!

8. Invest in Yourself: Budget for learning opportunities like courses or certifications that can boost your earning potential.

 9. Include your own: Do a little research or jot down ones you've learned throughout this playbook!

Shopping Hacks

1. Grocery Shop With a List ALWAYS: Stick to your list. Give yourself 1-3 "if I see something I didn't plan for, but really want" or "seasonal specialty" options to stay on track, but still get what you want.

2. Take Advantage of Cashback Apps: Use apps like Rakuten, Ibotta, or Fetch Rewards to earn additional money after you shop. Save and scan those receipts so you don't waste a dime.

3. Shop Discounted Stores or Farmer's Markets: They might not always have everything you're searching for. However, taking a trip to these stores first will always save you some coin.

4. Buy Generic Brands: Most store brands are just as good as the name brands for less. We're not just talking about food, but everyday products like skin care & hair care.

5. Shop Second-Hand When You Can: Thrift stores, Facebook Marketplace, and eBay can save you a boatload when you're looking for items such as furniture, car parts, gaming systems, household appliances & more.

6. Price Match: Stores like Target & Walmart offer price-matching, but very few customers take advantage of this.

7. Create a Shopping Ban List: Identify items you're prone to overspending on and commit to a temporary shopping ban.

Cutting Bills

1. Negotiate Your Bills: Call your provider or use an online service to negotiate lower rates for internet, insurance, or phone plans.

2. Switch Providers: Shop around for better rates on insurance, utilities, or cell phone plans.

3. Cancel Subscriptions You Don't Use: Do you really need Prime, Netflix, Hulu, Disney+, Spotify, Apple TV & Chewy? (You definitely need Chewy, but what about everything else?)

4. Switch to Energy-Efficient Light Bulbs & Avoid Using the "Big Lights": Lower your electricity bill in the long run with this habit.

5. Unplug Electronics When Not in Use: This reduces phantom power usage–and your bills!

6. Lower Your Thermostat: Save on heating by setting it 1-2 degrees cooler. Wash Clothes in Cold Water: This cuts down on energy costs.

Food and Dining

1. Use Flash Sale Apps: Apps like Too Good To Go offer discounted food from restaurants and bakeries at the end of the day.

2. Limit Dining Out: Craving some buffalo wings? Take a trip to the grocery store & pick up the best-quality ones they have. Not only are you getting more bang for your buck, but you can have buffalo wings the next day too.

3. Pack Lunch for Work: I know, I know, we all know about this one, but I want to emphasize the importance of $FREE.99. Plus, getting in the routine of doing this limits your waste & spoiled food.

4. Buy Groceries in Bulk: Stock up on staples like rice, beans, and Kraft mac & cheese at wholesale stores like Costco & BJ's.

5. Stick to Seasonal Produce: Seasonal produce is cheaper and fresher than out-of-season options, but also tastes so much better!

6. Plan for Meatless Meals: Save money by cutting out meat for a few meals. Try a cucumber salad & cheese bagel for lunch on days when you're not that hungry.

7. Avoid Pre-Cut Fruits and Veggies: Just cut them yourself. #1 the markup is crazy, and #2 most grocery stores will specifically use the over-ripe produce for their pre-cut options.

8. Double Batch Cooking: Cook double portions and freeze some for later, saving time and reducing the temptation to eat out.

9. Keep a Snack on Deck: Going out for the night? Bring some crackers & grapes in the Uber. Or get an order of wings & fries at the bar. Finish the wings, then stash the fries in your purse. Always keep a snack on you, especially if you're drinking, girl!

Lifestyle Adjustments

1. Use Your Local Library: You'd be surprised what they offer: free books, movies, and sometimes digital subscriptions like the local newspaper.

2. Cancel Gym Memberships You Don't Use: Invest in a walking pad. Try free YouTube workouts. Join a club that does outdoor activities. Moving your body is a free activity!

3. Sell Unused Items: Use platforms like Poshmark, Mercari, OfferUp, or Facebook Marketplace to declutter your home and earn some extra cash. It's a win-win!

4. Rent Out Space or Items: Rent your driveway on platforms like Spacer or your tools on ShareGrid.

5. DIY Household Products: Make your own laundry detergent by mixing borax, washing soda, grated Castille soap & essential oils. A huge tub of this could last you an entire year, yet cost a fraction of what you'd pay for branded detergent.

6. Take Staycations Instead of Vacations: Explore your local area instead of traveling far. The local mom & pops always have the best food anyways.

7. Repair Instead of Replace: DIY minor home repairs, deep clean those white sneakers, and revamp that dresser you want to replace. Let your creativity flow!

8. Use Cash for Fun Money: Take out cash for entertainment to avoid overspending on cards.

9. Create Your Own: Do a little research or jot down ones you've learned throughout this playbook!

☆ Upcoming goals & steps ☆

Goal name: ______________________________

Steps:

- ☐ ______________________________
- ☐ ______________________________
- ☐ ______________________________
- ☐ ______________________________
- ☐ ______________________________
- ☐ ______________________________
- ☐ ______________________________
- ☐ ______________________________
- ☐ ______________________________
- ☐ ______________________________
- ☐ ______________________________
- ☐ ______________________________
- ☐ ______________________________
- ☐ ______________________________
- ☐ ______________________________
- ☐ ______________________________

Goal name: ______________________________

Steps:

- [ ] ______________________________
- [ ] ______________________________
- [ ] ______________________________
- [ ] ______________________________
- [ ] ______________________________
- [ ] ______________________________
- [ ] ______________________________
- [ ] ______________________________
- [ ] ______________________________
- [ ] ______________________________
- [ ] ______________________________
- [ ] ______________________________
- [ ] ______________________________
- [ ] ______________________________
- [ ] ______________________________
- [ ] ______________________________
- [ ] ______________________________
- [ ] ______________________________

Goal name: ______________________________

Steps:

- [ ] ______________________________
- [ ] ______________________________
- [ ] ______________________________
- [ ] ______________________________
- [ ] ______________________________
- [ ] ______________________________
- [ ] ______________________________
- [ ] ______________________________
- [ ] ______________________________
- [ ] ______________________________
- [ ] ______________________________
- [ ] ______________________________
- [ ] ______________________________
- [ ] ______________________________
- [ ] ______________________________
- [ ] ______________________________
- [ ] ______________________________
- [ ] ______________________________

Goal name: ______________________________

Steps:

- [ ] ______________________________
- [ ] ______________________________
- [ ] ______________________________
- [ ] ______________________________
- [ ] ______________________________
- [ ] ______________________________
- [ ] ______________________________
- [ ] ______________________________
- [ ] ______________________________
- [ ] ______________________________
- [ ] ______________________________
- [ ] ______________________________
- [ ] ______________________________
- [ ] ______________________________
- [ ] ______________________________
- [ ] ______________________________
- [ ] ______________________________
- [ ] ______________________________

Goal name: ______________________________

Steps:

- [ ] ______________________________
- [ ] ______________________________
- [ ] ______________________________
- [ ] ______________________________
- [ ] ______________________________
- [ ] ______________________________
- [ ] ______________________________
- [ ] ______________________________
- [ ] ______________________________
- [ ] ______________________________
- [ ] ______________________________
- [ ] ______________________________
- [ ] ______________________________
- [ ] ______________________________
- [ ] ______________________________
- [ ] ______________________________
- [ ] ______________________________
- [ ] ______________________________

Goal name: ____________________

Steps:

- [ ] ____________________
- [ ] ____________________
- [ ] ____________________
- [ ] ____________________
- [ ] ____________________
- [ ] ____________________
- [ ] ____________________
- [ ] ____________________
- [ ] ____________________
- [ ] ____________________
- [ ] ____________________
- [ ] ____________________
- [ ] ____________________
- [ ] ____________________
- [ ] ____________________
- [ ] ____________________
- [ ] ____________________
- [ ] ____________________

Goal name: ___________________________

Steps:

- [ ] ______________________________
- [ ] ______________________________
- [ ] ______________________________
- [ ] ______________________________
- [ ] ______________________________
- [ ] ______________________________
- [ ] ______________________________
- [ ] ______________________________
- [ ] ______________________________
- [ ] ______________________________
- [ ] ______________________________
- [ ] ______________________________
- [ ] ______________________________
- [ ] ______________________________
- [ ] ______________________________
- [ ] ______________________________
- [ ] ______________________________
- [ ] ______________________________

Goal name: ____________________

Steps:

- ☐ ____________________
- ☐ ____________________
- ☐ ____________________
- ☐ ____________________
- ☐ ____________________
- ☐ ____________________
- ☐ ____________________
- ☐ ____________________
- ☐ ____________________
- ☐ ____________________
- ☐ ____________________
- ☐ ____________________
- ☐ ____________________
- ☐ ____________________
- ☐ ____________________
- ☐ ____________________
- ☐ ____________________
- ☐ ____________________

Goal name: ______________________________

Steps:

- [ ] ______________________________
- [ ] ______________________________
- [ ] ______________________________
- [ ] ______________________________
- [ ] ______________________________
- [ ] ______________________________
- [ ] ______________________________
- [ ] ______________________________
- [ ] ______________________________
- [ ] ______________________________
- [ ] ______________________________
- [ ] ______________________________
- [ ] ______________________________
- [ ] ______________________________
- [ ] ______________________________
- [ ] ______________________________
- [ ] ______________________________
- [ ] ______________________________

Goal name: ____________________

Steps:

- [ ] ____________________
- [ ] ____________________
- [ ] ____________________
- [ ] ____________________
- [ ] ____________________
- [ ] ____________________
- [ ] ____________________
- [ ] ____________________
- [ ] ____________________
- [ ] ____________________
- [ ] ____________________
- [ ] ____________________
- [ ] ____________________
- [ ] ____________________
- [ ] ____________________
- [ ] ____________________
- [ ] ____________________
- [ ] ____________________

Goal name: ______________________

Steps:

- [ ] ______________________
- [ ] ______________________
- [ ] ______________________
- [ ] ______________________
- [ ] ______________________
- [ ] ______________________
- [ ] ______________________
- [ ] ______________________
- [ ] ______________________
- [ ] ______________________
- [ ] ______________________
- [ ] ______________________
- [ ] ______________________
- [ ] ______________________
- [ ] ______________________
- [ ] ______________________
- [ ] ______________________
- [ ] ______________________

Goal name: ______________________________

Steps:

- [ ] ______________________________
- [ ] ______________________________
- [ ] ______________________________
- [ ] ______________________________
- [ ] ______________________________
- [ ] ______________________________
- [ ] ______________________________
- [ ] ______________________________
- [ ] ______________________________
- [ ] ______________________________
- [ ] ______________________________
- [ ] ______________________________
- [ ] ______________________________
- [ ] ______________________________
- [ ] ______________________________
- [ ] ______________________________
- [ ] ______________________________
- [ ] ______________________________

Goal name: ______________________________

Steps:

- [ ] ______________________________
- [ ] ______________________________
- [ ] ______________________________
- [ ] ______________________________
- [ ] ______________________________
- [ ] ______________________________
- [ ] ______________________________
- [ ] ______________________________
- [ ] ______________________________
- [ ] ______________________________
- [ ] ______________________________
- [ ] ______________________________
- [ ] ______________________________
- [ ] ______________________________
- [ ] ______________________________
- [ ] ______________________________
- [ ] ______________________________
- [ ] ______________________________

Goal name: ______________________________

Steps:

- ☐ ______________________________
- ☐ ______________________________
- ☐ ______________________________
- ☐ ______________________________
- ☐ ______________________________
- ☐ ______________________________
- ☐ ______________________________
- ☐ ______________________________
- ☐ ______________________________
- ☐ ______________________________
- ☐ ______________________________
- ☐ ______________________________
- ☐ ______________________________
- ☐ ______________________________
- ☐ ______________________________
- ☐ ______________________________
- ☐ ______________________________
- ☐ ______________________________

Goal name: ______________________

Steps:

- [ ] ______________________
- [ ] ______________________
- [ ] ______________________
- [ ] ______________________
- [ ] ______________________
- [ ] ______________________
- [ ] ______________________
- [ ] ______________________
- [ ] ______________________
- [ ] ______________________
- [ ] ______________________
- [ ] ______________________
- [ ] ______________________
- [ ] ______________________
- [ ] ______________________
- [ ] ______________________
- [ ] ______________________
- [ ] ______________________

Goal name: ______________________________

Steps:

- [ ] ______________________________
- [ ] ______________________________
- [ ] ______________________________
- [ ] ______________________________
- [ ] ______________________________
- [ ] ______________________________
- [ ] ______________________________
- [ ] ______________________________
- [ ] ______________________________
- [ ] ______________________________
- [ ] ______________________________
- [ ] ______________________________
- [ ] ______________________________
- [ ] ______________________________
- [ ] ______________________________
- [ ] ______________________________
- [ ] ______________________________
- [ ] ______________________________

Goal name: ______________________________

Steps:

- [ ] ______________________________
- [ ] ______________________________
- [ ] ______________________________
- [ ] ______________________________
- [ ] ______________________________
- [ ] ______________________________
- [ ] ______________________________
- [ ] ______________________________
- [ ] ______________________________
- [ ] ______________________________
- [ ] ______________________________
- [ ] ______________________________
- [ ] ______________________________
- [ ] ______________________________
- [ ] ______________________________
- [ ] ______________________________
- [ ] ______________________________
- [ ] ______________________________

Goal name: ______________________________

Steps:

- [ ] ______________________________
- [ ] ______________________________
- [ ] ______________________________
- [ ] ______________________________
- [ ] ______________________________
- [ ] ______________________________
- [ ] ______________________________
- [ ] ______________________________
- [ ] ______________________________
- [ ] ______________________________
- [ ] ______________________________
- [ ] ______________________________
- [ ] ______________________________
- [ ] ______________________________
- [ ] ______________________________
- [ ] ______________________________
- [ ] ______________________________
- [ ] ______________________________

Goal name: ___________________________

Steps:

- [ ] ______________________
- [ ] ______________________
- [ ] ______________________
- [ ] ______________________
- [ ] ______________________
- [ ] ______________________
- [ ] ______________________
- [ ] ______________________
- [ ] ______________________
- [ ] ______________________
- [ ] ______________________
- [ ] ______________________
- [ ] ______________________
- [ ] ______________________
- [ ] ______________________
- [ ] ______________________
- [ ] ______________________
- [ ] ______________________

Goal name: ______________________________

Steps:

- [ ] ______________________________
- [ ] ______________________________
- [ ] ______________________________
- [ ] ______________________________
- [ ] ______________________________
- [ ] ______________________________
- [ ] ______________________________
- [ ] ______________________________
- [ ] ______________________________
- [ ] ______________________________
- [ ] ______________________________
- [ ] ______________________________
- [ ] ______________________________
- [ ] ______________________________
- [ ] ______________________________
- [ ] ______________________________
- [ ] ______________________________
- [ ] ______________________________

Journal

Use this space to reflect, plan, or jot down thoughts. Revisit it whenever you need encouragement on your journey.

Journal

Use this space to reflect, plan, or jot down thoughts. Revisit it whenever you need encouragement on your journey.

Made in the USA
Monee, IL
13 August 2025

23275688R00103